Jest the Two of Us

Jest the Two of Us

A Humorous Look at His and Her Columns

SAMMY GRIFFIS & VICKI ELLIS GRIFFIS

Jokes and quips used in the last chapter have been contributed by Sammy and Vicki or their friends. Since the origin of some is unknown, we disclaim any ownership or control of rights to this unattributed material.

This book is dedicated

to our children and grandchildren

who allow us to share the funnies of their lives with the world, and who have endured our sometimes warped sense of humor with their heads held high and their therapist on speed dial.

Acknowledgements

Thanks to all our faithful newspaper readers and the Eons group who encouraged us to make this dream come true. Thanks for your patience, and we hope the wait was worth it.

Thanks to the late Ms. Mildred Roach who gave us our first writing encouragement and told Sammy the best thing he ever did for Celeste was marry Vicki and bring her there.

Thanks to the late Lois Lacy Lewis for reminding us of the importance of always writing everything down for posterity.

Thanks to the late Dr. Fred Tarpley, the Silver Leos Writing Guild, and David Broughton for reading, laughing in all the right places, and prodding us to finish what we started.

Thanks to Dale and Leslie Gibson of the *Celeste Star* for giving Vicki her start. Thanks to the *Wolfe City Mirror* for continuing our publications. Thanks to the *Greenville Herald Banner* for allowing Vicki to be a guest columnist.

Thanks to Lorane Mitchell of the *Celeste Tribune* for having us as feature columnists and asking us to keep them coming.

Thanks to Julie Medina for the cover design.

And last, but certainly not least, thanks to Patricia Ann Spurlock Vance and Sarah Roach Swindell for the many, many hours of reading, editing, and reading some more.

We could not have done this without you all!

Contents

Part One

In The Beginning

Genesis 1:27
So God created man in his own image, in the
image of God created he him, male and female.

1

I Am Sam, I Am

SAMMY

When I was born into this world, my great-aunt, Martha Griffis Marler, suggested that I receive the exact same name as my great-grandfather, Samuel Tate Griffis. Now, after already having to come up with names for my six older siblings—five of them boys, I'm sure my parents were quite relieved to have any idea of what to name me. Any name would do as long as they didn't have to think of one.

I broach the subject of my name because as I think about it, it really didn't matter what moniker I was saddled with, because, except for short stints in my life, I was hardly ever called by my given name.

When I was growing up, even my own mama had a hard time remembering what to call me. Almost always when she wanted my attention, this is the way it went: "Kenneth, Bill, Bob, uh, Jackie, uh, Stanley, uh, uh. . . ." By this time, she ran out of names and breath, so her voice just trailed off. It really didn't bother me, though. At least she hadn't called me Anita, which is my older sister's name.

Being raised in a very small town, it wasn't unusual for everyone to know you and your family. That's the way it was with me. Everyone knew me, but couldn't come up with my name. "Say, aren't you Red and Katie's boy?" folks would ask, referring to my dad and mom.

When I told them I was, they would say, "Well, I knew you were one of them Griffis boys, but I just didn't know which one."

Thank you. I appreciate the recognition.

About the only place I was called by my first name was at school, and that was only until about my freshman year. It was then, that except for a few who still called me Sammy, I became known as Tate, Griff, or dare I say it, *The Great Tate*. Today when someone addresses me by any of those names, I know they are either family or know me really well, so there is no need for me to put on any airs around them.

I graduated from high school, got a job, and finally had my own identity. That didn't last long, though. My friends and neighbors graciously selected me to serve in the United States Armed Forces where I was no longer Sammy, but Private Griffis. Talk about loss of identity, try being one of thousands of guys, all with a shaved head and clad in uniforms.

After separation from the military, I was beginning to be my own man. The new people I met called me Sammy or Sam. Hey, one guy even called me, Mr. Griffis. Okay, it was a police officer as he handed me a ticket, but it was something. Also, I must say I appreciated him calling me Griffis—not Griffith, Griffin, Griffins or Grittis.

Then it happened—I got married. And you know, I must have been a little deaf even back then because when I said, "I do," I thought I heard the preacher ask me, "Do you take this woman as your lawfully wedded wife?" but evidently he asked me, "Do you give up any semblance of having an identity of your own?" Because it was at that precise moment I became known as Vicki's Husband.

So much so that once a woman approached Vicki and me and struck up a conversation with Vicki. As the lady started to leave, she asked Vicki, "And how is your husband doing?" I don't know if she didn't direct the question to me because I was invisible to her, or she knew Vicki would probably answer for me anyway. I did feel a little insignificant, though.

And to really validate my anonymity, there was the time a friend's little girl saw me walking down the sidewalk and told her mother, "Look, there is VickiandSammy."

"No, that's just Sammy," the mother pointed out.

"Oh," the girl replied, "I thought his name was VickiandSammy."

Probably the worst case—no—it was definitely the worst case of mistaken identity ever associated with me happened at a football game many years ago when I had a full beard and fairly long hair. A little girl was sitting in the bleachers. She had seen me at church and paid attention to the lessons and pictures in Sunday school. As I walked up the stands, she elbowed her mother and whispered, "Look, Mommy, there's Jesus."

My identity crisis continued as I became known as my kid's Dad.

I don't much care now what I am called. I know who I am. I'm Vicki's husband, my children's dad, and my grandkids' Pop-Pop. I am happy with all my identities.

Still, I will admit I was a little encouraged when some friends of ours told me their little two-year-old grandson mentioned my name while he was playing. A few days later, I was over at their house and was excited as the grandmother pointed at me and asked her grandson what my name was.

His answer?

Why, it was Vicki, of course.

2

Never Swallow Watermelon Seeds

VICKI

The confusion started on the feather bed in my grandmother's living room—in the same exact feather bed where my mother had been born nineteen years before. My birth wasn't planned this soon, but it seemed to be the perfect way to start this thing I call life. Just like me to jump the gun and demand my grand entrance—two months early.

I sat at the feet of my grandfather as he spun that day many times. He would say, "Shorty, you were such a tiny little thing, we put you in the chicken incubator for two months after you were born." He laughed heartily, but I didn't get the joke, and told all my friends that I was placed in a chicken incubator for the first two months of my life. I was challenged on that event one day, and upon confronting my grandfather, I learned he had been joking. I was twenty at the time.

Being the baby girl of the family, I was accustomed to getting anything my young heart desired. All I had to do was shake my pretty blonde curls, flash my baby-blues, and say, "Pretty please—with sugar on it," and everyone melted. I guess one could say I started the princess movement way before the princess craze was cool.

I was about four when my mother's belly started growing suspiciously.

"Daddy, why is Mama getting so fat?" I inquired one day.

"Don't you worry your pretty little head about it. Your mama just swallowed a watermelon seed."

I was about to complain about how long it took to grow a watermelon, when Daddy said, "Shorty, you and your brother have to stay with your grandmother at the farm for a few days because your mama is about to have that watermelon, so we are headed to the hospital to get it out."

He winked at me like we shared some sort of joke, but I just clapped my hands and licked my lips—because I loved watermelon!

A few days later, Daddy came through the door with a tiny bundle wrapped inside a blanket. Mama was holding onto his arm, walking gingerly, and I swore to myself right then and there, I would never ever swallow a watermelon seed.

My daddy gently placed Mama into the rocking chair, and a sound that reminded me of the time we discovered several kittens in the corner of the barn came from the covering in her lap. The prospect of kittens excited me even more than watermelon.

I tiptoed over to see the tiny kitties. As Mama pulled back the blanket, I drew back in horror. My new pet looked a lot like a human baby with red hair! This was way too much for my little mind to handle. I looked over at my brother who didn't seem to be too interested in the whole turn of events. I felt sorry for him because he hadn't yet realized that he was being replaced by this tiny baby boy.

Then my daddy said the words that would forever change my life, "Come say hello to your new sister!"

Say what? Oh, no, that just isn't right! After all, if I was half as cute as I thought I was, why had they brought in this—this—*thing* to take my place? Something was dreadfully wrong! They switched the watermelon for a baby at the hospital, and my parents didn't even realize it. I knew I must rectify this situation and fast, but my suspicions fell on deaf ears.

As people came over to see this object of everyone's fascination, which horror of all horrors was sharing my room and blocking my spotlight, I heard, "My, you have grown," but to her they cooed, "Oh, you are the cutest little thing. You are a living doll. I wish I could just take you home with me."

I quickly answered, "Well, I am the good fairy, and your wish is my command." I tried several times to hand them her baby bag, which I kept fully stocked just in case someone took me up on the offer, but Mama just laughed and sent me out to play.

Meanwhile, they slobbered all over my sister, and as I headed out the door, I heard, "I wuv you so much! I could just eat you up!"

That first year was one of pure tolerance. I mean, how many times could one baby awake in the middle of the night because she wouldn't eat her supper? Geez, Louise!

I couldn't help but laugh every time she messed her diaper and filled our room with that awful smell.

"Mama!" I yelled, and she came running into the room. "See, aren't you glad I don't do that? Did you notice I went to the potty all by myself? Guess we'll just have to throw her away with the garbage. Anything that smells that bad must be ruined!" To which I was sent back outside to play.

About the time I thought I could stand it no longer, my dad took my brother, sister, and me back to the farm because Mama had swallowed another watermelon seed, and I knew nothing good could ever come of that.

Unbeknownst to my baby sister, she was about to be replaced. At least it took them almost five years to replace me. She was getting replaced after only thirteen months!

Well, Blondie came home to wild reviews. I have to admit, she was pretty darn cute, and my middle sister was turning into quite the fun playmate at times. But I wasn't so bad myself, and competition was the last thing a six-year-old fading princess needed.

After a few years, I resolved myself to the fact that I would never be the baby of the family again. I mean a swat on the soft side of the bottom did wonders to resolve all hair pulling, biting, and scratching, and what fun is hating someone without that?

But to this day, I won't eat anything but seedless watermelons. One can't be too careful.

Part Two

We're Tripping

John 14:31
Rise, Let Us Go From Here.

3

I'm Tripping

SAMMY

As I write this chapter, I am sitting in a motel room right outside St. Paul, Minnesota.

"What?" you may ask, "is a guy who doesn't want to ever be so far from home that he can't be back there for supper doing in Minnesota?"

It's a simple answer, really—I'm married.

The story began several months ago when my wife, Vicki, told me she wanted to go somewhere for our 40th wedding anniversary.

Oh, great, I thought, *she's going to want to go to a movie and probably to the Saltgrass Steak House*. But I said, "Sure, anywhere you want to go is fine with me."

I may have misspoken a little, because about an hour later, Vicki handed me about twenty pages of MapQuest printouts.

"What is this?" I asked "It's our trip!" she exclaimed. "Here, let me show you! We'll start by going to California to see Jeff. From there, we will go up the Pacific coast to Washington to see your family and then straight across to Wisconsin to see our nephew and niece.

"Of course, when we go through Oregon, I want to take a detour to see my friend in Sixes. After we leave Washington, I thought we would want to go to South Dakota to take a quick look at Mount Rushmore and drop by the Mall of America in Minnesota. It will be way fun!"

"Yeah, it is *way*, all right. . .*way* out of the question," I murmured as I flipped through the MapQuest pages.

"What about Kylie?" I asked referring to our youngest grand-daughter we kept every day.

"She starts to school the last of August. That's when we will go," Vicki said with a twinkle in her eye.

"Well, I'm sorry to disappoint you, Sweetheart, but we are *not* going on a 6,000 mile road trip. Not going to happen! Not now, not later, not ever—*never!*" I stated firmly.

So on the 3rd of September, one week after Kylie started to school, I loaded the car with a month's worth of luggage, and we began our trip.

Maybe here would be a good time to confess, I have a touch of acrophobia, the fear of heights.

I was fine through Texas, New Mexico, and Arizona. We were traveling on I-10, when our son, Jeff, called asking where we were. I told him, and he advised us to take I-8, or The 8 as they call it in California, and we could save an hour or two getting to his house.

"Does it have any high mountains we have to cross?" I asked apprehensively.

"I think there may be one little section that is a little scary for you. But no, not really any that would bother you that much," Jeff said.

A few hours later, if I looked to either side of the road, I was staring down three or four thousand feet. I kept my eyes straight on the pavement so I wouldn't freak out. Seeing a bridge straight ahead, a fairly long bridge with nothing underneath it but air, I felt the uneasiness creeping up from my stomach and into my chest—I was in the beginning stages of a panic attack.

Now, picture this:

I am on the bridge and out of the corner of my eye, I catch a glint of something and turn to see what it is. It is the camera Vicki is holding up to take pictures. That wouldn't have been so bad—but I am not making this up—she is driving!

"What the heck (or something like that) are you doing?" I scream. "Are you trying to kill us? Put both hands on that steering wheel and get us down this mountain, now!"

"But it is so beautiful, I want a picture. . . ."

"Never mind that!" I yell as I grab the camera. "Just get us on lower ground," I plead.

Silence never sounded as good as the ride down that mountain.

Soon we were in San Diego, headed north to Jeff's house. There are some things in life too traumatic for your brain to handle. I think that is what happened to me, because the next thing I knew, we arrived at my son's condo, and it was 9 p.m. We were tired, but happy to see him. We sat up awhile and talked, then Jeff suggested we all retire for the night, because he had to work the next day.

So the next morning, after a tour of Jeff's office and warehouse, he told us he was going to try to take off early, and we could meet up with his girlfriend, Jenn, and go down to the ocean and do some boogie-boarding and pitch some horseshoes on the beach.

Ah, the fun had just begun. Be still my heart, the Pacific Ocean— did I mention I have just a tad of hydrophobia, the fear of water?

4

Love Is Blind

Vicki

How did I ever pull this off? I thought as we sailed out of town for a six-thousand mile road trip. The trip was number one on my bucket list, and I couldn't believe my husband, Sammy, consented to go. No matter why he did, I was going to get out of town as fast as I could before he changed his mind.

After a few hours, we hit the eighty-mile-an-hour speed limit in or around Abilene, and I soon found out why they have it set so high. You had better make sure you fill up your tank and empty your bladder before you get on that stretch of road, because you won't be able to do either for miles to come.

I laughed as Sammy yelled in desperation, "Hurry up and get me to the rest stop before my water breaks!"

We drove eighty-miles-an-hour so we could slide into the next town just in time to fill up and empty!

There wasn't much to see but sand and cactus for miles, but when the scenery began to change so did my husband's zeal for this trip. His mood wasn't so bad through the beautiful white sands, and he even humored me and turned around into the scenic view atop a mountain, as he called it—I called it a hill—on Interstate 8.

When I tried to take pictures while driving over the scenic 8's version of The Grand Canyon—well, let's just say he wasn't being nice when he grabbed the camera from my hand. And to make matters worse, he did it before I got any pictures.

So I pouted, sighing and letting a tear or two drop as we descended the mountain in silence, making sure Sammy was getting the full impact of my hurt feelings. As we coasted to flatter ground, his blood pressure almost returned to normal, and he became a kinder, gentler husband—until he realized we hadn't timed it well—at all. Now it was his turn to pout.

Yes, arriving in San Diego, California, as the sun was going down, I never mentioned it was probably that stop at the White Sands which put us behind schedule—not on my life!

Only ninety-minutes from my son's condo, I don't know what led me to say, "I can do this," other than the fact it seemed so silly to stop at a hotel that close to Jeff's place—and hey, there was still a little daylight when I spoke the words—and ninety minutes in California is nothing like ninety minutes in Texas—so actually, this wasn't my fault.

When we pulled onto the 5, all daylight suddenly disappeared, and this little country girl found herself driving on a five-lane highway in the dark. I discovered something way too late—I am night blind—not just a little, but totally! I wondered about this a few times coming home from Greenville a little late. But then I knew where I was going, and there was only one lane going one way straight to home.

Here I was in the Twilight Zone, and all I could do was follow the tail lights of the car in front of me, hoping against hope, it was going to Jeff's condo. Nope, it led me into a tunnel-like road with concrete close to my car on both sides—the one thing in this life of which I am most afraid. I gripped the steering wheel until my knuckles turned white and never took my eyes off those tail lights, except for brief glimpses trying to find my way out of the dreaded carpool lane.

About that time, I fell in love with a woman who would become my best friend for the next five-thousand miles. My new-found love was the voice behind the GPS system. Now remember she is a woman driver, so she didn't tell me to take the right lane until we were right on the exit, and I had to cross four lanes of traffic. But she did get me there. I closed my eyes—they weren't doing me any good anyway—and prayed no one was beside me. I steered toward (and just barely made) the right exit. Thank God, He had my back—and front—and side.

I saw the sign that read Newport Beach and looked over at Sammy to see why he wasn't screaming at me. I stifled a chuckle when I realized he was dialing Jeff as fast as he could. No way, no how, was he going to believe either woman driver until he was safe and sound and parked in Jeff's garage.

Jeff talked me to his street, and I was excited when I pulled into what I thought was his driveway. Not being able to see the numbers on the houses, I was just about to get out when I heard Jeff from the speaker phone.

"That is *not* my condo!" I heard him yelling at me via his dad. "Did she not see me standing in the middle of the street yelling and waving my arms?" he asked, excitedly.

"No!" we both answered in unison. Did I mention Sammy is night blind, too?

"Incredible, just incredible," I heard Jeff mutter as he climbed into the driver's seat and pulled us safely into his garage.

Needless to say, Jeff wouldn't let us drive the whole time we were there. But like a good mother, I didn't remind him we still had five-thousand miles of driving in front of us—all by ourselves. Looking at his travel-worn parents, he had enough to worry about for now.

5

Boogie-Boarding Mama

VICKI

One thing I have learned during my travels to California to see Jeff is my body isn't as young as it used to be. That's the trouble with going to visit thirty-somethings—they know no fear and have unlimited energy. *Heavy sigh*! I remember those days, but this wasn't one of them.

Jeff woke up bright and early in the morning, at 5 a.m. Now in my world 5 a.m. didn't exist! The happiness in his voice came through as he said, "Get up, Mama. It's another fun day! Come on, I want to show you the ocean. We are going boogie-boarding!"

I didn't know what boogie-boarding was, but I would rather find out after a couple more hours sleep. Before I could tell him I wasn't ready to get up, the look on Jeff's face told me—we were going to the ocean—now!

"Do you mind if I wear my bikini?" I asked him, thinking that would surely deter him and give me another hour or so of rest. The panic on Jeff's face, as he beckoned Jenn to help him, was priceless.

Jenn, not one for controversy, shrugged her shoulders and gave him a look back as if to answer, *She is your mom. You deal with it. I'll just stand back and laugh.*

I prolonged their agony as I took my time getting ready. I slowly walked out of the bathroom, and I don't think I have ever seen such looks of relief as they had on their faces when they saw I was wearing a cover-up with a bikini painted on it. Much to Jeff's joy, I never took it off at the beach, not even when boogie-boarding!

So here we went, ocean or die—an omen of things to come—but, I am getting ahead of myself.

Our feet sank into the hot sand, and the heat burned all the way to the bone. Muscles already aching from climbing the stairs to Jeff's condo several times now protested with each step.

"Okay, Mama, you dive into this ten-degree water, take this little piece of styrofoam, hold onto this tiny piece of string, walk out to that ten-foot wave, jump on top of it and ride it back to shore at fifty-miles-an-hour, holding your breath for five minutes."

Well, that isn't exactly how he described it, but that was my reality of it.

Much to my surprise and theirs, I rode the first wave all the way to the sand. Of course, it was about a three-foot wave. But it was a good start, and I was energized, ready to take on the big one. I walked out deeper and rode a four-foot wave in. *This is great fun*, I thought. I was up to about ten-miles-an-hour, and I would have been perfectly happy to do that all day.

But Jeff had other ideas, "Mama, come on. Quit kidding around. You have to come out *here*."

Now I am 5'5", and he was standing in over six feet of water.

"I don't think so!" I hollered, but he couldn't hear me. So I walked closer to him to let him know I wouldn't be coming out into water over my head. The water was at my chest now, but I was hanging onto the boogey-board, safely staying afloat.

This isn't so bad, I thought. I happily waved to Sammy, who was watching safely on shore and mouthing something while he frantically pointed behind me. When I looked back, I saw the massive wall of water five-feet above my head—too late! I didn't exactly make it atop the boogey-board—but I did hang onto it for dear life—not that it did me any good. All of a sudden, I wasn't atop the wave, but under the water, not knowing which way was up.

First, I rolled around and around like a yo-yo, then jerked up, then upside down, and finally, slammed hard into the sand on the beach. When I finally opened my eyes, I saw the guys standing over me. I lay there coughing like a beached whale. When they heard life stirring out of my lungs and ascertained I was still breathing, they high-fived each other, as if they had saved my life.

I heard, "That was amazing—that was awesome—I think you turned every which way but loose!" and heavy laughter.

"Ya think?" I said sarcastically as I got up and checked myself for injuries. I found nothing hurt but my pride. I had sand and salt embedded in every crook and cranny of my body—places I didn't even know I crooked or crannied.

"Want to go again?" Jeff asked me excitedly. "You have the hang of it, now. Look, here comes the biggest wave of the day."

I was thinking more in the direction of *I want to lie down on my beach towel and take a nap till it is time for us to leave*. However, when I could finally see through the sand in my contacts, I saw something wicked in Jeff's eyes—like kite-surfing, bungee jumping, in-line skating down the I-5 Freeway—and fear clenched my heart.

"Okay, we can do this again tomorrow. How about a game of beach horseshoes? Then we can go bowling," he said

"Yes!" I rolled over, every nerve in my body screaming. That sounded like something nice and safe. Jeff handed me the horseshoes, which weighed about one-hundred pounds each and told me I had to throw them about a quarter mile and circle a metal pole for something called a ringer.

Well, that wasn't how he described it, but that was my reality of it.

After the game, my arms were now on their last legs (and my legs were on their last arms) but at last, we walked back to their condo.

"Let's go bowling," Jeff and Jenn said in unison, full of vim and vigor. I looked at them in disbelief, groaned and said, "You go ahead. Right now I am trying to figure out how I am going to climb this one flight of stairs," and the look on my face told them I wasn't kidding.

"I'll race you!" they yelled as they headed up the stairs three at a time.

Heavy sigh! I remembered those days, but today wasn't one of them.

6

The Texas Two-Trip

SAMMY

The weekend was here—one last chance to go to the ocean before we left my son's place in California to go to Washington. I couldn't wait to get to the beach. I found I loved boogie-boarding, which is like surfing, except you lie on the board. Yep, there is something fearful, yet exhilarating as you sit on the beach and watch your wife and son stand on their head on top of a wave as the ocean tosses them and the boogie-board high into the air.

Seriously, I had no intention of boogie-boarding myself. However, I had promised both of them I would at least get in the ocean. Although I suffer from a little hydrophobia, I summoned all my courage, went down to the water's edge, stuck my finger in the Pacific Ocean, determined it was indeed wet, turned and walked back up the beach. Promise kept.

The next morning we said goodbye to Jeff and headed north. About an hour later, we were in Los Angeles. Do you know what amaxophobia is? Well, I think I may have just a tad of that. It's the fear of traffic. If I didn't have it before, I had it when I got through there. Oh, my gosh! How could this many crazy drivers be assembled in one place? We zigged—we zagged—we went—we stopped. We hoped—we prayed—we made it! Finally, we were out of L.A. Praise the Lord!

We hit the 101—see, I now spoke Californian. We were making good time until we started getting into the mountains. We ascended. We descended. We went 25 mph as we twisted and turned our way through the beautiful Redwood Forest on our way to Oregon.

"Aren't these trees awesome?" Vicki asked for the tenth time.

"Yes," I groaned. "And I am going to see one up close and personal if we don't find a rest stop soon!"

Finally, we saw a sign indicating a rest stop was only a few miles down the road. Forget the mountains, trees, rivers and other scenic surroundings; I only had eyes for the rest stop.

By this time, Vicki's daily consumption of about two gallons of tea had kicked in, and we were feeling the same pain. We slid into the rest stop parking lot, jumped out of the car, and dared anyone to get in our way.

Breathless and in agony, I made it to the restroom just in the nick of time. I let out a high-decibel, *AH-H-H-H*, as I felt the victory of relief. I guessed folks had never heard anyone express that much joy just by using the urinal. As I turned around, everyone was staring at me as if I was some weirdo. Then one of the guys pointed to the Texas logo on my t-shirt, and they all nodded knowingly as I walked out to get in the car.

At last, we were out of California and into Oregon. It was dusk when we arrived at our motel in Sixes to meet our friend Lurell for supper. She treated us to a nice meal and good conversation.

It was getting late, so we agreed to meet for breakfast the next morning. As we made our way back to the motel, Vicki commented about the nice view of the ocean we had from our room. I, however, had noticed the signs on the way in that warned: *Possible Tsunami Area*.

Vicki slept peacefully that night as I lay there—eyes wide-open—waiting for the first wave to come crashing through the window.

Somehow, we survived the night, met Lurell for breakfast and said our goodbyes. Washington bound! I couldn't wait to see my brother and sisters and their families.

There was only one little problem I faced. Have you ever heard of gephyrophobia—the fear of bridges? Well, I have just a smidgen of that, and we were coming into Portland where we had to cross the mighty Columbia River to get into Washington.

We were fighting our way through Portland traffic when I saw it, a bridge rising high above the river. I felt apprehension as we approached. Now we were on it, but except for the elevated blood pressure, rapid heartbeat, and sweaty palms—and a short stint in the floorboard—I did fine.

We made it across to solid ground, and just as my vital signs were returning to normal, what did I see? Another bridge, higher than the one we had just crossed. *Man, ain't we got fun?*

We made it to the other side, and my hyperventilation subsided when I realized we were finally in Washington, where in a few hours we would be at my Brother Jack's place.

At long last, we arrived. It was great to be there! We were going to be in the same place for a week! I wouldn't have to cross a high bridge, go up a mountain, or hunt a restroom for a week. Oh, happy days were here again!

My brother's place was kinda small, so he asked a friend to set up a Winnebago for us to use during our stay. The time was getting late, and we were tired. Asking if it would be all right if we called it a night and went to bed, Jack said, "Sure," as he showed us to the motor home, "but the space is smaller than what you are used to."

I was pleasantly surprised when we arrived at the campsite. It was one of the larger ones. When we went inside, we found it to be roomy and comfortable. *Well*, I thought, *at least claustrophobia won't be an issue.*

We were out in two seconds, sleeping soundly, when I was awakened by a sound in the living area of the RV.

"Did you hear that?" I whispered to Vicki.

"No," Vicki answered sleepily.

I guess I had just been dreaming, I decided and went back to sleep. A short time later, I was awakened again by a knock on the door. I sat up in bed and listened intently. There it was again, another knock!

"Did you hear *that*?"

"No!" she answered, somewhat agitated by my waking her.

I got up to investigate the knocking, put my ear to the door and asked, "Who is it?" No answer.

"Is anyone there?" I asked again. Nothing. I mustered up enough courage to open the door to look around. I didn't see anyone or anything. *Oh, my gosh*! I thought to myself, *I hope I am not experiencing a bout of spectrophobia*.

"Spectrophobia?" you ask. Well, you are just gonna have to look that one up.

7

Coasting—Or Not

VICKI

Saying goodbye to your son when you don't know when you will see him again is always hard. I couldn't look back as he stood waving from the sidewalk. Tears filled my eyes, and as I have had to do so many times, I thought of something fun to keep from totally losing it.

The beauty of coastal California would help, I smiled. "Sammy, let's take the coast all the way to Washington," I beamed.

Sammy, not being one to just say, "That sounds like fun," protested for several minutes while I turned onto the 101 headed straight for the California shore.

But where was the beautiful coast I was supposed to be seeing to get my mind off my broken heart? All I could see were walls and trees—and oh, my gosh—what was that? Graffiti?

Where were we? Surprise! *Welcome to L.A.* the sign read.

101-110? That could be easy to mix up, couldn't it, especially with someone yadda yadda yaddaing in the background?

Traffic squeezed in on both sides of us, and in the dark recesses of my mind, I thought I heard Sammy saying, "Pull over."

"What?" I asked him, "You have to go to the bathroom in the middle of graffiti-covered territory?"

I could tell by his face he wasn't kidding. Why hadn't I stopped back in Long Beach where it was pretty and clean and safe? *We hadn't been on the road long enough, that is why*, I reasoned. Knowing in my heart this was a fool thing I was about to do, turn off the freeway I did.

We took a turn here and there, looking for a better neighborhood, but looking over at my husband squirming in his seat, I knew he couldn't wait much longer. Seeing the graffiti get bolder and more frequent, it didn't look like the neighborhood was going to get any better, so I pulled into a 7-11 in the midst of a sea of tattoos and bandanas, or as the sign read *Skullcaps*! Now that sounded ominous.

"You coming with me?" Sammy asked.

Duh? I started to answer, but he was already running to the store. I didn't appreciate how fast I could run until I realized he was in no condition to wait for me, and I sure as heck wasn't staying in the car all by myself.

One of the suspects of my imagination opened the door for me and smiled. I felt ashamed of myself until I noticed the large knife inside the scabbard on his belt buckle. I swallowed hard and thanked him. Now it was my turn to almost wet my pants!

We made it in and out of the store, and no one tried to kill us or anything. Still, we sighed with relief as we left the graffiti-laden overpasses behind and pulled back onto the freeway. Headed to the 101, Sammy realized we were headed straight to San Francisco.

Now in our marriage, I have put my husband through many things he had done because he loved me, but making him cross the San Francisco Bridge wasn't going to be one of them. He decided—well, demanded—we take a detour. Little did we know it would take us a whole day to keep from crossing a 1.7 mile bridge!

I started to protest, but all Sammy could think of was the article he had read which said the San Francisco Bridge had two hundred and fifty pairs of vertical suspender ropes, and the last suspender rope hadn't been replaced since May 4, 1976.

I called my daughter to tell her about our diversion. "Besides we wouldn't have gotten to see the Arco Arena, home of the Sacramento Kings, and I wouldn't have wanted to miss that," I laughed sarcastically into the receiver.

After an overnight stay, we were on the road to Sixes, Oregon. Driving through miles and miles of twenty-mile-an-hour hairpin curves, I told Sammy, "I will *never* think mountains are beautiful again!"

As we entered the Redwood Forest, I wanted to stop every fifteen feet to take pictures, but the tourism marketers are smart. They didn't make one place to pull over until you got to a tourist trap where gas was $5.85 a gallon! Thankfully, we had enough gas to get us to the next town, or so I hoped.

The beauty of the trees took my breath away—for the first sixty-miles. After one-hundred-twenty-miles of them, I just wanted to see daylight again. We had passed a sign which read *Drive-Thru Trees*, and I said to Sammy, "Yea, yea, I get it—trees and trees and trees."

Only after we stopped at the tourist trap did I realize there were actually trees wide enough for you to drive through.

"You didn't know that?" Sammy asked me.

"Yeah, like you knew that and didn't explain it to me—oh, you sorry sucker. You did know that and just didn't want to stop! That is just wrong."

Oh, well, knowing my husband as well as I did, we weren't turning around and going back, so I said, "I want to stop at the house built inside a tree."

I assumed he would stop. I was pointing at the attraction as he drove right on past. I pouted a second, but was soon laughing and clapping as I saw the sign *Leaving the Redwood Forest* as we drove into the sunshine.

Finally, the coast of Oregon was coming into view, and it *was* gorgeous. We called our friend, Lurell, and she gave me directions to the hotel. The phone rang as we were putting our things in the closet.

It was Lurell. "Where are you?"

"In the hotel."

"But I am at the hotel, and I don't see you."

I heard a gasp on the other end of the line. "Ugh, I think I gave you directions to the wrong hotel," she cried.

Over supper that night, we laughed about her senior moment sending us to the wrong hotel. We had already paid and put all our things inside the one she had led us to. The *other* hotel was where her granddaughter worked—but oh, well, it was something I could hold over her head *forever*.

After a good night's sleep—they didn't have internet service, so what could you do but sleep, right?—we met Lurell again for a breakfast of stomped-on eggs, a term I had never heard before. When they arrived, I realized they were what we called over-hard in Texas.

Lurell and I had decided to go to the Lighthouse before we left, but the persistent ringing of the phone changed Sammy's mind. Brother Jack was on the other end. First he insisted, "You need to come on if you are going to get here by dark!"

But I wanted to see the Lighthouse, so I said, "I will risk it."

Then he said, "There is a lot we need to do to get you settled into the trailer I have arranged for ya'll to stay in."

I wasn't budging, so he tried guilt, "If you don't come on, I am paying park rent for nothing."

Guilt works with me every time.

Sammy seemed surprised I had agreed so easily to leave as we left Lurell standing in the restaurant parking lot with a sad look on her face. I didn't tell her till I was out of earshot from Sammy, but I had only agreed to leave early so I would have an excuse to come back—*because I didn't get to see the Lighthouse.*

"No, don't mess with the wife, Sammy. You didn't marry *no* fool."

8

Two Down—Two To Go

SAMMY

*W*hen we last talked I told you about arriving in Washington, staying in a RV at my brother Jack's place, hearing things going bump in the night, and wondering if I had spectrophobia; which, by the way, is the fear of ghosts. Even though I thought there may have been some paranormal stuff going on, I decided to go to bed, not worry about it, and try for a good night's sleep.

After all, what you gonna do? When it comes to ghosts, who you gonna call?

Waking early the next morning before anyone else was up, I decided to take advantage of the nice weather to go for a walk on a trail my brother had shown me the evening before. Stepping outside into the crisp air, it was almost like walking into a picture postcard. I could clearly see Mt. Rainier, one of the most beautiful mountains (from a distance) there is. Walking across a wooden bridge spanning a small river, I heard water running below me, so I walked over to the rail and looked down. The stream moved gently around the huge rocks in its path, and as I stood there gazing at the river, listening to the soothing sound the water made as it continued downstream, I was energized and filled with anticipation for the day.

Vicki had expressed her desire last night to get an early start today—this usually meant that we would get started, oh, around 10 or 11 a.m. So to my surprise, she was up, rip-roaring and ready to go when I got back about 8 o'clock.

After a leisurely breakfast and lunch with my sisters, Vicki and I rested for a while, then met Jack and his girlfriend for a walk down to the river, hoping to see salmon swimming upstream to spawn. Large rocks protruded from the river bank, making it fairly hard to walk. As we made our way gingerly over the sharp stones, I heard a loud, *Oooooh*! coming from the direction Vicki had headed. Thinking she had spotted a salmon, I turned just in time to see her feet airborne as she fell backwards on the rocks. I admired her, though. She busted her backside big-time and still managed to hold her camera up in the air, protecting it as a mother would an infant. Forget breaking the back—forget the arms—forget the legs—forget the neck: *Save the pictures*!

We helped Vicki to her feet, and after walking around for a minute or two, she seemed to be okay. We decided to call it a day and went to our RV to spend a quiet night of reading and watching television.

The next day, we spent with my 84-year-old Aunt Frances, who I hadn't seen for twenty-three years. I had never visited my oldest brother Kenneth's grave, so we drove to Chehalis where he was laid to rest. Any death is a tragedy, but his was especially so. He had served two tours in Vietnam only to return home and die a few years later—pulling from his neighbor's driveway across the road to his. He was killed instantly when a dump truck hit his pickup. We paid our respects and left.

Aunt Frances suggested a casino to cheer us up. I didn't want to go, but my brother and my aunt *made* me. Being one to always respect my elders, I grudgingly went with them. We walked in and asked the concierge what we were supposed to do. He sent us over to the cashier's cage to buy a card in the amount we wanted to spend. When we arrived at the counter, a pretty blonde cashier asked to see our driver's license.

"Oh, I see you guys are from Texas," she said.

"Yes, Ma'am," I replied in my best Texas drawl, "I reckon we are."

"Well, right in front of you is the twenty dollar tables, to your left are the five dollar slots, and just so you know, down at the other end of the casino are the high stakes tables. Now, how much would you like on your card?"

"Uh, well, I guess ten dollars," I answered.

I could almost read her thoughts as she handed me the card: *Well, big Texas spender, how many oil wells did you have to sell to shell out that much cash at one time?*

But she asked, "Is there anything else I can help you with?"

"Yes, Ma'am, where are the nickel slots?" I responded rather weakly. I turned and started walking in the direction she pointed, my Texas bravado decidedly diminished. I returned to that same window later, however, and smiled smugly as I handed the girl my cash ticket requiring her to pay me a crisp twenty dollar bill. *Take that, baby,* I thought as I took the money, and, *Oh yeah, don't mess with Texas!*

After a whirlwind week which included a family picnic, where I got to see nieces and nephews (and great-nieces and nephews) I hadn't seen in years, it was time to continue on to my nephew Joel's place in Ontario, Wisconsin.

We had completed two of the four legs of our trip, but it was time to begin the third leg of our journey. The next morning we said goodbye to everyone and made our way to I-90, heading east to Idaho. In the next week, we would continue east as we traveled through Idaho, Montana, Wyoming, South Dakota, Minnesota and Wisconsin. As has been previously noted, I am not a big fan of mountains because of having a little acrophobia. I hoped the worst was behind me—I hoped—but, baby, I hadn't seen anything yet.

9

Hit The Road, Jack

VICKI

"Oh, my gosh! Yes, I'll pray. I promise," I told Jack's girlfriend. She had just informed me Jack was in ICU after being shocked back to life due to congestive heart failure. The doctor told them he would need surgery, and it could go either way. I was shaking as I hung up the phone. *Why, we were just there*, I cried. Isn't it amazing how fast your joy can change to pain?

After I explained to Sammy what had happened to his brother, without saying a word, we both got really quiet and started praying silently, hoping for a miracle.

We couldn't help but think back to when we visited his home.

"Remember when we got there, and Jack ran to greet us, followed by half the dogs in the neighborhood? Of course, we had gotten lost trying to find his house," Sammy laughed. We could still see him standing outside, cell phone to his ear, waving us in.

Jack was the King of the Road at his trailer camp, we soon discovered. His home was the place to be.

"Hey, Jack, got any matches?"

"How about a cup of coffee, Jack?"

"Need anything, Jack? I am headed to town."

His friends would continuously pop in. They didn't seem to have much or need much. If anyone had anything, everyone else was welcome to it. It was one big, continuous camp out.

When Jack walked us to the RV where we would be staying, first one person, then the next got in line behind us. By the time we reached our spot, the whole camp wanted to see the new kids on the block. The RV was great—full bed, bathroom, and cable TV, and we even got a little up close and personal time when we passed each other in the hall. A little closeness never hurt a couple, especially while on vacation. Jack explained the camper had everything a person could need. I was thrilled—until I tried to boot up my computer. *No internet? What? A week without the internet—how would I survive?* I wondered, but I sucked it up. *I can do this*, I told myself, hyperventilating into a paper bag.

I took it one day at a time, and somehow I made it. We had envisioned a week sitting outside, resting, reading, and relaxing. *Not!*

Bright and early the next morning, we walked into the bakery and restaurant where their sister worked. We watched Jack play the room. Everyone's face lit up as he stopped at a table. He had more jokes than Henny Youngman, and his presentation was hilarious.

"Remember the day Jack took us sightseeing?" I reminded Sammy.

"Oh, yeah, how could I forget?" Sammy laughed.

Jack had a quaint little town he wanted to take us to so that we could experience the ambience of the region.

"It is just right down the road," he said as he drove us through dirt roads, waterfalls, and ghost towns. Before we knew it, we were headed up something that resembled what we had driven two thousand miles through—more mountains!

Now, I had personally informed Jack that Sammy wasn't fond of mountains or bridges, and I thought I had made myself perfectly clear. Next thing I knew, we were climbing a very steep mountain, and I was incredulous that Jack would take us there.

We had been driving over an hour, and Sammy leaned over and whispered, "Just down the road in Texas is a little different than just down the road in Washington!"

What we saw brought us both to terror. There in the middle of the winding, narrow, mountain road was a rickety one lane-bridge hanging over a canyon, and there was no place to go but over it.

I started to admonish Jack, when the worry lines on his forehead told the story—Jack was lost—he was as panicked as we were. We slowly crossed the bridge, feeling the wind beneath the car all the way, only to find the backside of a hair pin-curve in front of us.

"Jack, we need to turn around!" I cried, meaning at the next available place. It was there I learned a valuable lesson. *Be specific when making demands*, because he turned around right there!

As the SUV edged precariously close to the rim of the canyon with no visible railing, I gripped the door handle and started praying no one would come around that curve.

Of course, if they did, the impact would hit full-force on *my side* of the car and send us into the ravine below. I was pushing that invisible brake as hard as I could.

Sammy was way too quiet, and I feared he had had a heart attack as his eyes were closed—and he was almost in the fetal position.

Jack eased forward, then back several times. Finally, he was out of danger and headed back the way we came—back over the one-lane bridge and down the mountain towards home.

"I think I have had enough ambiences for one day," Sammy said as he straightened up in his seat. Sadly, we never did find the little town Jack had been taking us to.

"Do you remember the picnic?"

"Do I?" Sammy laughed.

On the way home that day, Jack talked non-stop about the family picnic we were to have Sunday, the day before we were to leave. So when Sunday came, we were expecting about fifteen family members. I couldn't hide my surprise when Jack told the cook in the deli he needed a one-hundred-piece chicken meal. I wondered why in the heck he was getting so much chicken.

I would soon learn his family consisted of much more than blood kin. I pictured Jack as the Pied Piper as he told everyone we saw on the way there, "My family is having a picnic down at the park. Why don't you join us?"

Soon this one and that one were in line behind us once again. As we snaked to the picnic tables, I saw his family shaking their heads. Our family picnic had grown from fifteen to fifty.

"We should have known," they said in unison as they saw us all coming over the bridge. "That's our Jack!"

But shortly, Jack had us all laughing, and you would have thought we had known each other forever. There were stories about the friend whose son was in Nashville recording another hit, and a neighbor who serenaded Aunt Frances, much to her bewilderment.

"Secretly, I think she was flattered," I quipped.

It was clear to us all, everyone was brought to this place because of Jack, and he couldn't have been happier.

The phone rang again, bringing us back to the somber reality of today. Jack had survived the open heart surgery and another surgery for a pacemaker, and we did the Hallelujah Dance for our miracle boy.

Sammy joked, "Why didn't you schedule the heart attack while we were there so we could be with you?"

I teased him, "Jack, you have got to get well so we can meet you in Vegas. We need you to be our tour guide. And if you don't mind, that trip, we'll let Jesus take the wheel."

Sometimes you have to laugh to keep from crying.

10

Geezers, Geysers, Lakes And Quakes

SAMMY

We were headed east on I-90 toward Idaho— destination Wisconsin. The plan was to take our time, stop whenever we felt like it, do a little shopping and sight-seeing, and get to Wisconsin whenever we got there.

We were on the road about three or four hours, however, when a common male syndrome kicked in. You know the one: *Get from point A to point B as fast as you can. Do not stop. Do not look side-to-side. Stay focused and get to where you are going.*

It didn't seem as if we had been driving all that long before we were out of Washington and into Idaho. It was just a hop, skip and jump across the panhandle of Idaho and into Montana where we stopped for the night.

The next day we were cruising down the road in Montana, when I started seeing signs touting Yellowstone National Park. Vicki had said she wanted to go there, but I was hoping she had forgotten about it. Each time I saw a sign, I would divert her attention, hoping she wouldn't notice them. I guessed it would be interesting to go see it, but I wanted to get on down the road. She never mentioned it, so I thought my diversionary tactics were working—that is until we had to stop for gas.

The tank full, we went inside for a drink and some snacks. As I walked out of the store, the first thing I saw was a huge sign with an arrow pointing to Yellowstone. I quickly started talking to Vicki, pointing to some stuff in the window, trying to keep her from seeing the sign. I had her by the arm, guiding her so I actually had us walking backwards to the car. People were stopping and staring. They had never seen folks our age doing something akin to the moonwalk in a convenience store parking lot. Michael Jackson would have been proud.

All of a sudden, Vicki stopped. It was as if some sort of subconscious phenomenon came over her. Her head spun around on her neck almost like Linda Blair's little girl character in *The Exorcist*.

"Look," she said, pointing, "that sign says that road goes to Yellowstone. There's a roadside map. Let's go over and take a look."

Walking over to the map and determining Yellowstone was about two hours or so away, she pleaded with me, "Let's go, Sammy. We might not ever have another chance."

"Hmmm, Vicki, you know how far down the road we could get in two hours?" I asked.

"Yes, I do," she answered, "It will get us right to Yellowstone. Come on, you know I've always wanted to see the Old Faithful Geezer."

I laughed at her pronunciation and said, "If it's an Old Faithful geezer you want to see, I'm right here beside you. But if it's the Old Faithful geyser you're looking for, I guess we have to go to Yellowstone."

Quicker than I could close the door, we were headed to West Yellowstone, Montana, to spend the night.

The next day found us inside the national park looking for Old Faithful. As we drove along, we saw wisps of smoke rising here and there. We soon discovered it was actually steam from geysers. I thought Old Faithful was the only geyser there, but geysers (and geezers) were everywhere.

We made our way to the main event to watch Old Faithful erupt. We weren't allowed to get too close to it, so we sat on some benches quite a distance away. After reading the brochure telling us the time each eruption would take place, there it was, right on time, spewing its steam high in the air.

The sight was pretty awesome. I have to admit the geezer enjoyed the geyser.

I'm glad Vicki made. . .um. . .encouraged me to go see it.

After Old Faithful, we decided to leave the park. I looked at the map and determined we should go out the east side of it into Wyoming. Heading east, we passed miles and miles of burnt trees. I remembered hearing and seeing about the great fire on the news, but I never realized what a daunting task the firefighters bore trying to contain the forest fire. It was an eerie sight.

Lost in the magnitude of it. . .I. . .*uh oh*. . .we were starting to climb again. I looked at the map. We were headed into the Absaroka Mountains. I looked closer at the map and saw we would be going up over eleven thousand feet—eleven thousand feet! Let's see, five thousand two hundred and eighty feet in a mile. . .eight plus eight. . . carry the one. . .add the fives. . .hey, wait a minute, we were going to be over two miles up in the air—in a car—on narrow roads with hairpin curves—with no room for error—with Vicki driving!

My acrophobia kicked in full throttle. I'm serious. I didn't think I would make it! I freaked out to the max. Every time I looked out beyond the road, I felt I was going to pass out.

And to top it all off, Little Miss Sunshine was over there saying, "Oh, look! Isn't God's world beautiful? Isn't this an awesome view?"

"I'm sure it is," I gasped in between my deep-breathing exercises, "but I'll have to take your word for it. It's kinda hard to see. . . you know. . .me lying down in the seat and all." I finally felt the car going downhill, and I stole a glance at the road just in time to see us approaching a very sharp curve—a curve where something had run through the guard rail. Oh boy, I felt way better now.

We were still very high up, so I looked down at the floorboard until I finally felt the car leveling off. When I looked up, we were driving beside one of the most beautiful lakes I had ever seen. I saw a sign informing us it was Quake Lake.

"That's a unique name. I wonder why it is called that?" I asked Vicki.

Before she could respond, I got my answer. There was another sign telling us we were in an Earthquake Zone. Oh great, we made it off that mountain, and now an earthquake was probably going to drown me in Quake Lake.

But by the grace of God, we made it completely out of the mountains *and* the quake zone. I looked at the scenery we were passing through and asked Vicki, "Look, isn't God's world beautiful?"

"What are you talking about?" Vicki asked. "There is nothing here but miles of ol' flat prairie land." "I know," I replied, as I smiled and sighed with relief.

"I know! Isn't it awesome?"

11

We Just Keep Going. . .And Going. . . And Going

SAMMY

We were rolling along in Wyoming headed for South Dakota to visit Mt. Rushmore. It was a pleasant drive, but I kept a wary eye on the Big Horn Mountains off to our left. I felt pretty good though, because it looked as if we would remain in the valley and be able to travel around them. I actually relaxed and enjoyed myself as we drove alongside the Big Horn River. Kinda lost in my thoughts, I pondered all the history connected with this part of the United States. Not too far north of here, back up in Montana, was where Custer's Last Stand at the Battle of Little Big Horn occurred.

All of a sudden, the road turned left, and I was jolted out of my daydream. We were headed straight for more dad-blame mountains. A particularly ominous looking one lay ahead—and yep, you guessed it—that's the one we had to cross. I will spare y'all the details of another mountain adventure. I will say it was. . .oh what is the word that best describes it? Scary. . .horrible. . .horrendous. . .terrifying? Yes, that's it—*terrifying*!

I don't know for sure, but I thought at one point I heard the girl's voice on our GPS unit joining me as I screamed, "Vicki, watch out! Slow down! Don't ride the brakes! Be careful!"

Well, we finally made it out of the mountains, but had made horrible time. Driving a little longer than usual to make up for the lack of distance we had traveled, we were cruising down the highway, and it was getting dusky-dark.

Vicki said, "Look at all those buffalo up there."

"Where?" I asked, straining to see them.

"Up yonder at the foot of those hills. I hope they are still there when we get nearer to them."

I looked closer to see what she was talking about. "Oh, they aren't going anywhere," I responded.

"What makes you so sure?" Vicki asked.

"Because," I answered, "those are round bales of hay wrapped in black."

After that, we both decided maybe we had better find a place to stop for the night.

The next day we arrived in South Dakota and headed to Mt. Rushmore. It wasn't too far from Rapid City, just south of the little town of Keystone. We drove up to see it, and there it was—Mt. Rushmore—the mountain I had seen in pictures and read about all my life.

I thought we could probably see it from the highway. But no, you had to go up some more mountains before you could even get a glimpse of it. Although I didn't exactly enjoy the drive up to it, I had to admit it was pretty cool to see it in person.

Staying the night in Rapid City, we arose fairly early the next morning. Bound and determined to make it to Minnesota before we stopped driving for the day, we put the pedal to the metal while travelling down I-90 on flat terrain and putting the miles behind us.

Before we knew it, we were almost all the way across South Dakota, so we pulled into a diner right before Sioux Falls. It was in this diner, I encountered one of, if not, the worst waitresses ever.

We walked in. No one spoke to us, so not knowing what else to do, we seated ourselves in a booth. The waitress, a late teen to early twenties young lady, was sitting at the counter. She glanced our way, but didn't acknowledge us.

Vicki and I looked around, trying to get someone's attention to take our order. Finally, she strolled over to our booth, and by her facial expression and demeanor, made no secret of the fact she had just as soon we hadn't shown up. Without saying a word, she dropped two menus on the table and returned to the counter and sat down. After a while, she came back to ask if we were ready to order. We ordered hamburgers and tea. Again, not saying a word, she left to give our order to the cook, brought us our tea, and sat back down at the counter, never looking our way again until the burgers were ready.

The place was nearly empty, but our order took a fairly long time. Finally, the waitress brought us the burgers, never offering to refill our tea, and started to walk away. I looked at my burger. It was composed of just meat and bread.

"Uh, miss," I called to her, "y'all forgot to put any tomatoes, lettuce or pickles on my burger."

"You didn't ask for them," she replied, rolling her eyes.

"Well, where I'm from you have to ask to have them left *off* your burger," I explained.

"You can have them, but it will cost extra," she informed me, smacking her gum.

"Oh, just forget it," I replied and choked down the hamburger. We hurriedly finished eating and had to ask for the check. Taking it to the cash register, I discovered that our waitress was the cashier. She didn't say one word when I paid our tab.

I thought about telling her how horrible her attitude and service were, but decided that just because she didn't act like a lady, it shouldn't keep me from acting like a gentleman. Besides, if someone had held me down as they obviously had her and stuck a key ring through my lower lip, a thumb tack in the side of my nose, and a couple of nails in my eyebrow, I might be mad at the world, too.

We happily left Sioux Falls and crossed into Minnesota, making it about halfway to Bloomington before we stopped for the night.

Vicki had plans—big plans for tomorrow. We were going to where every man in the world wants to go. We were going to a mall—not just any mall—The Mall of the Americas, the largest mall in the U.S. of A. Oh joy, oh joy. Be still my heart!

12

Oh, What A Ride

VICKI

Credit card waving in the air, I ran through the Mall of America yelling, "Charge!" Overloaded with packages, I carried some to the car and raced back for more.

That was the scenario Sammy imagined as he ventured into the largest mall in America with a wife grinning like the Cheshire Cat— The Mall of America, every woman's dream—every man's nightmare.

"How awesome is this, Sammy?" I yelled. "Can you believe there is a roller coaster in the middle of a mall?"

His expression made it abundantly clear that riding that monstrosity with him in tow was *not* happening. I felt a little tug at my heart picturing my son and daughter and little grandchildren squealing with glee if they were here, and how much they would enjoy riding it with me. My eyes landed on the Tilt-A-Whirl, and I ran to get a picture, leaving Sammy standing there shaking his head, confirming what I had known for over thirty years: There would be no amusement rides with him, *ever again*.

"Look, one of the characters is named Austin," I gave it one more shot. The Tilt-A-Whirl having the same name as our grandson phased him none whatsoever. He wasn't budging. We sat and watched awhile, and my mind drifted back to the only time in our long marriage Sammy had ridden an amusement ride with me.

Thirty-three years ago at Six Flags over Texas, the kids pulled their daddy into the waiting line, begging him to ride the Mini-Mine Train. Being the wonderful father he was, he agreed. It wasn't until we climbed that first steep hill and started going round and round, head popping first this way, then that, when he *and I* realized he had been duped. We were on the Maxi-Mine Train, and I could see—he was *not* a happy camper. I never could convince him I wasn't in on their little scheme, and I don't think he talked to us for two weeks after that. From that day forth, he has been happy to sit on the bench and watch us ride to our hearts content.

The sound of the Tilt-A-Whirl zooming very close to my head brought me back to the present. I sure wasn't about to ride that spinning maniac alone, so we headed to another floor more suitable for adults—Legoland. The exhibit featured giant dinosaurs made out of Legos, yep, my granddaughter's favorite thing. I never thought I would say it in a million years, but I was getting homesick.

After looking around for another hour or so, I decided the stores were the same ones we had back home, just bigger and more expensive. As we sat in the middle of that gigantic mall drinking an Iced Caffè Latte, I looked over at Sammy and whispered something to him he never expected, "Let's go."

"Go, as in leave this place—or go, as to another floor?" he asked hesitantly, looking around at my empty shopping cart, suspecting this was too good to be true.

"Go, as in let's make like a tree and leave," I mocked his favorite saying. The look of surprise, excitement, and exhilaration on his face surpassed any I had seen on this trip so far.

Actually, it dawned on me that he agreed to that stop after we had already spent most of our traveling budget. He was much smarter than I gave him credit.

But so am I. You just can't win with a wife who has traveling in her blood. I had put back some money for this mall, so I silently hid it away and made a list of all the things we would do with the kids and grandkids when we brought them with us on our return trip next year.

One last thing Sammy had worried about was getting from Minnesota to Wisconsin without crossing over the Mississippi River Bridge—yep, the same eight-lane steel-truss arch bridge which carried 140,000 vehicles daily and catastrophically failed during the evening rush hour on August 1, 2007, collapsing to the river and riverbanks beneath, killing thirteen people and injuring 145 others—*that* Mississippi River Bridge. I had looked online and assured Sammy they would route us elsewhere, as the bridge hadn't been restored. Well, sometimes the information on the internet isn't always current.

"Uh, oh!" I gasped when I saw the cranes and chains and machinery alongside the bridge—too late! We were now crossing over it. I knew I was in deep trouble if and when we ever got to land with no water underneath it. Heck, Sammy might never speak to me again.

I took my eyes off the road just for a second to see just how much murder there was in his eyes. Much to my surprise, he was taking pictures of the river below. I gave him a confused look, and he beamed once we were safely across, "I wasn't worried at all. You can bet this bridge is now the safest bridge in America."

"You've come a long way, Baby," I laughed.

I had secretly calculated the savings from shopping which could be used to spend a couple of days at the Treasure Island Casino and Resort in Redwing, Minnesota. Thinking on a Tuesday night we should have no trouble getting a room, we were amazed to see the acres and acres of cars in the parking lot when we pulled in.

The girl at the front desk informed us their 500 plus rooms were all filled. Sammy was giving me that *I can't believe you didn't make a reservation* look as she confirmed there was no room for us at the inn. Who would have thought?

"Is there a convention?" I asked.

"No, it is like this every night," the indifferent twenty-something replied, looking at us like we were truly from Mars and Venus.

"Evidently, news of the bad economy crisis has by-passed Redwing, Minnesota," I defended our lack of reservations, my voice growing shriller with each roll of her eyelids. Sammy, having seen that side of me before, steered me back to the car before I clouded up and rained all over her and made her walk home in the mud.

Hoping to find a hotel by dark, by the time we made it out of the parking lot, I realized once again we were too late. Visualizing another episode like San Diego, we decided to pull into the first hotel we saw, but did I mention I was night blind? So blind that I missed the driveway to the hotel, and not caring to travel ten miles down the road to the next turn around, I whipped the Nitro around for a U-Turn.

Yep, that is when I heard Sammy scream. As we bounced and clunked and were thrown first this way and then that, I grasped too late—the median was not *painted* yellow. In fact, it wasn't a median at all, but a six-inch high curb, and I had straddled it, much to Sammy's chagrin.

I really couldn't hear what he was screaming—due to the noise the car was making as I tried to spin out over the hump—and come to think of it, that was probably a good thing.

Sammy slammed out of the car, and I started praying. I think the only thing that kept me alive that night was Sammy's realization that there was no way he could drive back home all by himself!

The power of prayer worked! Sammy determined that a miracle had indeed occurred. There was no damage to the car or the curb.

As I studied his face in the headlights, I had to chuckle as I thought, *Well, I did get you to go on a wild ride with me after all.*

But of course, being the wise little wife I am, I would never say anything like that out loud. . .not on my life.

13

My Eyes, Texas, Are Upon You

SAMMY

*Y*ippee-Ki-Yi, Yippee-Ki-Yay!
We made it to my nephew Joel's house in Ontario, Wisconsin. That was to be the last stop for us before we headed home. We planned on staying there for two or three days, then we would find our way to I-35 south and roll on to Texas. *Why, I could almost smell the cow patties.*

Don't get me wrong, we looked forward to our visit with Joel and his pretty wife, Gisela, and their three children, Jacqueline, Janice and Joel, Jr., but we had been traveling for twenty-four days, and I was a little antsy to get back to the Lone Star State.

Driving up to their beautiful home on several acres sitting above a little valley which afforded a wonderful view from their patio, I was reminded their place was once a working apple farm with a retail store for the apples, but Joel had suspended the operation since he lost his whole labor force to graduation. Yep, his kids.

Joel—or as Vicki embarrassed him by calling her nickname for him in front of his newspaper reporter friend— *J-o-e-y*—and Gisela proved to be great hosts. I saw the wheels turning in Vicki's head that maybe we should stay longer.

After Gisela served us a big breakfast, we headed off for the Cranberry Festival. Now I've never thought of anything associated with cranberries being very festive. But here we were, smack-dab in the middle of acres and acres of crafts. . .cranberry ice cream. . . crafts. . .cranberry jelly. . . uh. . .crafts. . .cranberry candy and. . .well, crafts. Really, though, it was great fun, and we thoroughly enjoyed the day—especially since Vicki only bought a purse or two—which was somewhat of a miracle in itself.

Ontario is right in the middle of Amish country, so the next day Joel showed us around the area. The countryside was beautiful in that part of Wisconsin, and the Amish houses and barns added to the attractiveness. Each place is self-sufficient. They have their own live-stock, chickens, and gardens to supply their needs. From the young-est to the oldest, everyone seems to be contributing to the running of the farm. The men work the fields, and the women work around the house and manage their little shops where they sell crafts, eggs, homemade cookies, ice cream and bread. You know what they say about how to keep women down on the farm. . .well, I did notice all of them were bare-foot. However, I didn't really check out the pregnant part too closely.

We watched the men harvest corn with a horse-drawn cutter and load it by hand on a horse-drawn wagon. Vicki remarked, "Oh, it would be so nice to live like they do!"

She was so impressed with the life-style; she pulled her air-con-ditioned, late-model car over to the side of the road, lowered the electric window, took a picture of them with her digital camera, and called someone on her cell phone to tell them the virtues of the simple life.

I, however, remembered my days growing up on the farm pulling corn, hauling hay, and picking cotton. It might have been simple, but it was hard. My back started hurting just thinking about it.

The next morning Joel served us coffee out on the patio. It was a bittersweet day. Today, we would be leaving for home. As much as I had been anticipating getting home, I had such a good time it was kind of hard to leave. Besides, Joel was already firing up the grill to cook steaks for lunch.

While we were waiting for lunchtime to arrive, Joel, Jr. offered to take me for a ride on his four-wheeler to see the back part of their land. Vicki gave a loud, ominous laugh as he popped a wheelie, and I hung on for dear life.

What was I thinking, getting on the back of an ATV with a teenager?

Joel and I headed down the road and soon cut off onto a trail that took us through thick brush and low-hanging limbs, which Joel, Jr. didn't seem to see as we were slapped first on one side and then the other.

As we made our way through the trees, I saw something ahead dart across the trail. It was pretty far from us, but it looked to be black and didn't seem to move like a deer. I asked Joel, Jr. if he had seen it. He nonchalantly said, "No, but it was probably a deer or maybe a small black bear; so we probably should turn around, just in case."

Gulp! I agreed. I wanted to get out of there because I knew what I had seen. It wasn't a deer or a bear. . .it was. . .it was. . .Sasquatch! That's right. I had seen Bigfoot! Dang, a Kodak moment and me without a camera.

After lunch, Vicki and I said goodbye to our Wisconsin family. We backed out of the driveway, and as we turned onto the road, I flashed them a Hook 'em Horns sign, yelled, "Yee-Haw," and headed out—the wrong direction!

We snuck back through Ontario, hoping Joel hadn't ventured into town to see that his poor aunt and uncle had spent an hour lost.

Finally, we dipped back over into Minnesota to connect with I-35 and turned south. The next two days we spent traveling through Iowa, Missouri, Kansas and Oklahoma.

During the last thirty days, we had crossed the Colorado, Columbia, Mississippi, Missouri, and Big Horn Rivers, just to name a few, but not a one of them was as beautiful as the one we crossed last—the Red River.

Oh, and there's that big, beautiful, wonderful sign. The sign that says, *Welcome to Texas*. That meant we were about an hour and thirty minutes from home.

Soon we turned onto the gravel road to our house. Pulling around back onto the driveway to the garage, Vicki and I both leaned back in the car seats and took a deep breath of relief. We looked at each other, smiled and high-fived. We had made it! We had traveled six thousand miles and only had six near-death experiences. But now we were home.

We each grabbed a suitcase and walked through the house straight to the bedroom. Dropping our baggage, I flopped into my recliner as Vicki fell back on the bed.

"Oh, it is so good to be home. I am *never* leaving this house again!" Vicki vowed.

"I thought you had a cruise planned for Cozumel with the Spurlock girls early next year," I stated.

"Oh yeah," she answered, "I mean after that."

Part Three
All In The Family

Genesis 33:5
And he lifted up his eyes, and saw the women and the
children, and said, "Who are those with thee?" And he said,
"The children which God hath graciously given thy servant."

Proverbs 13:22
A good [man] leaveth an inheritance to his children's children.

14

Kung Pao Chi Ting—Not

VICKI

"Chinese food! Heck, yeah!" I shouted when the ladies from our book club suggested we go eat at the Chinese food buffet after seeing a movie. You see, my family doesn't do Chinese food. In fact, the first and last time I tried steering them toward it was almost thirty years ago. Needless to say, it wasn't my greatest success story.

Sammy has been a beans and taters man all his life. Would I dare suggest Chinese food to him? Of course not. What kind of wife do you think I am? So eager for the experience, I got our friends to do it.

So when they asked Sammy, and I quickly responded, "We would love to!" Sammy gave me *the look*. But I didn't give in to his commanding frown for once. I was so sure if my family tried it, they would like it.

My resolve did start to weaken, however, when we walked in and all three members of my family reached up and held their noses, simultaneously. It was my turn to give them my look and whisper loudly, "*Stop it!*"

They knew by my raised eyebrow, I meant *or else*!

The waitress seated us, and the silence was deafening. I could see Sammy and the kids suspiciously eying each entrée as they were brought to the tables around us. Our friends, taking charge of the uncomfortable lapse in conversation, called the waitress over and ordered for us. I was thankful because I had no idea from looking at the menu what was in items such as Bang Bang Ji or Kung Pao Chi Ting, and I didn't dare ask until Sammy had at least tasted it.

After twenty minutes of taking a drink, and the waiter refilling our glasses, I knew if the food didn't arrive soon, we were headed for barbecue—again.

I could tell my husband was growing very impatient for the waiter to deliver our *'we knew not what'* so I leaned over to Sammy and said, "Isn't this fun? I bet you are going to love it!"

I knew he wasn't keeping a very open mind when he looked back at me, rolled his eyes, and whispered, *"I'll take that bet."*

The hurried waiter sat a large bowl of Egg Drop soup in front of my crew. Stefani immediately asked, "What is all this stuff floating around in it?"

Jeff held his nose, again.

Our friend, Allen, giving me the *'I will get us out of this. Just hide and watch'* wink, ladled some of the watery mixture into our individual bowls and said, "Oh, that is fish eyes and hen droppings."

Stefani turned green and asked to be excused.

As I recall, we couldn't get any of them to try it, even though Allen spent the next fifteen minutes trying to convince them he was only teasing.

When the waiter brought a plate of fried egg rolls, I sighed. I knew they would like those. They liked anything fried.

But Allen, taking great delight in torturing my family, couldn't restrain himself. He bit into the egg roll and teased, "Aw, cabbage and fried worms. Love it. Love it. Love it."

This time, his wife, Lisa, and I simultaneously kicked him under the table—hard!

Sammy was actually quite a good sport as he picked one up and took a bite. Love was not a word I would use to describe how he felt about it, not even close to like. But for the sake of the children, he ate every bit of it and encouraged them to do the same. Their lips stayed tightly sealed.

The main course finally arrived, and the sight of green bell peppers and steak brought smiles to my family for the first time since we walked in the door. Jeff beamed, took a bite of what looked like a potato and announced "Ugh, they aren't done!"

I explained it wasn't a potato. It was a water chestnut. As we giggled, our son put down his fork, and we could tell by his scowl that he was *not* finding any of this funny.

A short while later, Sammy admitted he was enjoying the restaurant—well, the company anyway.

Jeff piped in, "I would have loved it if I had never had to take a bite of anything."

Finally, something arrived that brought smiles—fortune cookies. As we all opened ours, took out the little slips of paper with fortunes typed on them and read them out loud, happiness was restored to the faces of my family and friends.

Sammy read his first: *A journey of a thousand miles begins with a single step.*

I was about to make the analogy of our adventure today, but decided to lay low on that one.

We got the biggest laugh when our son opened his cookie, and it read: *To stay healthy, eat more Chinese food.*

He actually smiled, then put his finger in his throat and gagged.

The kids finished the meal by eating their cookies and asking if they could have seconds. See, I knew they would like Chinese food once they tried it.

We started to part ways, our friends walking to their car with three takeout boxes of *our* leftovers, when Allen, who had tormented everyone with his warped sense of humor, turned to Sammy with a mischievous twinkle in his eye and asked, "You want to eat here again next week after church?"

Sammy looked at him as if he had lost what little sense he had left (the twinkle totally lost on him) and replied, "I think I have had enough Chinese for a while. But I would love to go out and eat with you all again next Sunday. Just remember, I'm from Texas, and I prefer my food American style."

I leaned against the car and watched my wacky friends and family, smiling as they bantered back and forth with Sammy—the kids running and playing chase in the parking lot.

I had saved my fortune cookie, so I opened it and read the words on the small, white slip of paper: *Quit searching. Happiness is sitting right in front of you.*

I beamed. It surely was, even if they didn't like Bang Bang Ji or Kung Pao Chi Ting.

15

Mommy, Kiss It And Make It Feel Better

VICKI

Sitting happily watching SpongeBob SquarePants get himself out of another pickle, my six-year-old granddaughter, Katelyn, groaned that her tummy was hurting–and hurting bad.

She cried, "MiMi, help me! I don't feel so good."

Touching her forehead, I was surprised to feel the burning heat. Just a few minutes before she had been fine, and now she was seriously ill.

A quick call to her doctor suggested we come to the office right away. Usually I would have a fight from my little one, who always kicked and fought her way out of going to the doctor, so I was surprised when she yelled, "Hurry, MiMi!"

So I did!

I carried her out the door and into the car in less than a minute. Fifteen minutes later, she was rushed back in the examination area to await the doctor. She didn't protest much when the nurse took her temperature and her blood pressure. As they handed her a cup, I smiled for the first time since she said she was sick. "Take this cup and go to the restroom. Hold it under your urine stream until it is three-quarters full," the nurse instructed. This was more than her little mind could grasp. She looked at me and crinkled her nose.

"Uh, uh, that is too gross!" she declared, but she walked her little walk of shame to the bathroom carrying the cup behind her back.

Getting the deed done was much easier than trying to get her to let the nurse draw blood. It reminded her why she hated going to the doctor in the first place—needles. No way were we going to get it without a fight. It took three nurses and me to hold her down, but we finally got enough to send for a diagnosis.

Katelyn colored while we waited for the doctor to return with the results. When the doctor walked in, the look on her face shouted, *Alarm!* Now, seeing panic on a doctor's face when your six-year-old granddaughter is lying on a gurney isn't a good thing.

"She needs to get to the hospital as soon as possible as her white blood count is 15,000 and it should be 4,000," our family doctor said as gently as she could so as not to frighten Katelyn—or her grandmother.

A quick call to my daughter and son-in-law, and we were headed to Rockwall. My sick grandgirl moaned loudly, and I kept reassuring her everything was going to be all right, as much to calm my nerves as hers.

Picking her up gently and carrying her into the hospital, I reluctantly handed her over to her parents. I had been caring for and nursing her for hours, so my heart hurt a little when the emergency room nurse said, "Only her parents may come back with her."

As the doors closed, she looked at me and held out her little hand, not quite understanding why I wasn't coming with her. I blew her a kiss, fought back tears, and went to meet up with Sammy and her three-year-old sister to await further news.

Before we could get back to the hospital, Stefani called to let me know Katelyn had been transported by ambulance to Children's Hospital for an emergency appendectomy. "Mom, the nurse had informed me it could be hours before they know anything because they want to run their own tests. I'll call you when they are ready to take her to surgery, and you can come then. The emergency room is a nightmare right now, so it is best you and Daddy wait at the house."

Just like that, I had gone from caretaker to grandparent. And like a good one, I fought the urge to get in the car, break into that emergency room, and let those doctors know I had kept her almost every day of her life, and I needed to be there with her!

Instead, I settled by the phone for one of the longest nights of my life, praying without ceasing.

When the phone finally rang about 4 a.m., I was thrilled to hear my daughter say they had decided Katelyn didn't have appendicitis after all, but a bad kidney infection. The doctor had given her an IV of antibiotics, and they were awaiting release orders.

When they arrived home, Katelyn looked like a war refugee, having been put through so many tests. The little cup for a urine sample seemed like a sweet memory now.

After tucking her safely into her own bed, far away from the needles and cat scans, IV's and enemas, tears rolled down my daughter's cheeks as the dam of emotions burst.

"Mama and Daddy, as I held my little darling's tender, bleeding little fingers, I realized I hadn't stopped and held her for weeks. With several setbacks at work, I have been too busy—*too busy*—now that I look back. It occurred to me while sitting by her side, holding her hand and listening to her, rubbing her bruises and giving her lots of kisses, that I had given her the standard night time hug and peck, but not the true heart-felt appreciation of thanking her for being her.

"When she asked me to lie beside her, I took the time to tell her how much she means to me. She looked at me and said, 'Mommy, you are so beautiful.'

"Looking at myself with mascara smeared and hair frazzled, I couldn't imagine what she was seeing, but my husband was looking at me the same way—they were seeing my heart, which at that moment had become beautiful. I was no longer worried about chores, getting the house clean, homework done, getting baths, getting her to bed on time, or picking out outfits. I was only thinking of her—the great things about my little six-year-old girl.

"When I tried to get her to drink sixteen ounces of the barium mixture, it wasn't easy. Her fiery stubbornness ignited. She wasn't going to drink it, and no amount of prodding was working. Her daddy came over, and she calmed a little. That lasted about five minutes. He was trying to use reason, which made sense to me, but not to her.

"A thought popped into my mind, 'What would Mama do?' I so needed you there at that moment to tell me. But then it hit me! I heard you whisper, '*Bribe her.*' So that is what I did! She had for so long wanted a Gameboy. There was no way I was going to pay a hundred and fifty dollars for such an item for a six-year-old. *Never*! I mean, who does that?

"Mom's do that! They do it when it means the most. Now was definitely the time to do it. You know why? At that moment, it wasn't about the money. It was about my child's health, and I knew it was the one thing that would make her drink that nasty barium. It worked! No prodding, just the promise of a simple toy did the trick.

"This started me to thinking. I *do know* my little girl—the way only a mom can know one. I *had been* listening, because most wouldn't have known that conversation we'd had hundreds of times about a pink Gameboy and a Princess game. Most wouldn't know the way she works, what motivates her, what makes her happy or sad. That is what a mom knows. I began to smile, because I knew that through the chores, housework, outfits, and baths, I was listening, engaging, and getting to know my daughter.

"And Mama, I remember another thing—she never gets one-on-one time with us. I couldn't think of the last time it was just the three of us. Even through her illness, I think she noticed.

"It was just us paying special attention to our middle child. We took this time to reflect on her, focus on her, and give her all our energy. That was a blessing. Even through the pain, I was appreciating this alone time to just listen to her stories, her words, hugs, and without interruption, I was able to be just what she needed at that moment and time.

"God gives us gifts in the strangest form. But I see those hours and days as a gift because it renewed my spirit as a mother and has made me stop to reflect what is truly important—being my kid's mother! To stop and not look at my children as a whole, but reflect on each of them individually."

As Stefani finished, she wiped her tears which had flowed like a river. All of a sudden, she was my little girl again. I hugged her for dear life. When I looked at her, I saw my granddaughter's parent. My little girl loving her little girl with only a love another mother could know, and a peace came into my heart as I realized that is just how it is supposed to be.

16

Spongebob And A Hemi

SAMMY

"Baby, why don't you sit down and rest awhile?" Vicki asked our youngest granddaughter, Kylie, hoping against hope.

At three years old, she was being quite rambunctious, and to be honest, the respite was needed more by us than by her. The request, however, went unheeded as she continued with her—shall we say— spirited play.

In an effort to reach a peaceful solution to the problem, Vicki asked again, "Honey, why don't you sit down? You can watch *SpongeBob SquarePants*."

When she mentioned SpongeBob, I looked at the clock. It was twelve forty-five.

"No," I said, "*Max and Ruby* is on right now, *SpongeBob* won't be on until one." I stopped for a moment and thought about what I had just said.

Oh my gosh, I wondered, *is this where I am in life, knowing the schedule of the Cartoon Network, Nickelodeon, and the Disney Channel by heart?*

To make matters worse, when SpongeBob is mentioned, I can't get the catchy theme song out of my head. I sing it over and over until I'm half-crazy.

I have to be honest, though, I like *SpongeBob SquarePants*. To me, it is one of the funniest shows across all genres on television. As you get to know the characters, it's even funnier.

You don't know the characters? Well, I can help. Let's see, there's SpongeBob's best friend, Patrick. I think he is a starfish. Squidward is his co-worker, and his boss is Mr. Crab. Then there is Sandy and Plankton—but I digress—I was talking about where I am in my life.

I see people younger than me trying to pick up votes to become president of the United States. I'm picking up Little Mermaid dolls off the floor (which comes on at two-thirty, by the way.)

There are folks who are curators of huge art museums. My art consists of water colors, finger paints and markers. I never knew a kitchen table could look so pretty, you know, multi-colored like that and all.

There are CEO's making multi-million dollar decisions. Me? My big decision for the day is whether it will be corny dogs or spaghetti for lunch?

Folks meet and have coffee to discuss politics and Wall Street. I have my coffee with a three-year-old and discuss her pets: Kitty, Bun-Bun, the rabbit, and a hamster named Fluffy.

Now, don't get me wrong, I am not saying if I wasn't keeping my grandchild, I would be some big shot doing great things. I have long known I will never be rich or famous. Realistically about all most of us can hope for is to have a decent house and car, so we might as well learn to be satisfied with what we have.

Still, sometimes I think about how my life would have been if I had transferred to another location instead of leaving the company where I was employed when the plant I worked in shut down.

Instead of watching *The Wonder Pets*, 12 p.m. . .why, by now, I would probably be the. . .and if I didn't have to sit here and share my nachos while we watch *Blue's Clues* (3 o'clock each weekday), I coulda been a. . . .

Nah, to tell the truth, I don't think I would change a thing about my life now. I don't believe there is an *etched in stone* blueprint for success. What success means to one person might not mean a thing to another. At this point, I can tell you what it means to me, though. It's a brown-haired, brown-eyed little girl who asks, "Do you know how much I love you, Pop-Pop?"

"No," I answer.

"This much," she shows me as she stretches her arms as wide as she can.

"That's a lot of love," I say, and we both giggle. "Now, let's go pop some corn so we can watch Scooby-Doo," (Tivo'd from 6 o'clock last night.)

We settle down on the couch. I put my arm around Kylie, and soon she is fast asleep. As I look around the room I see all the things I have been blessed with, but it is when my eyes turn back to my grandgirl sleeping that a warm feeling envelopes me.

Man, I think to myself, *I am one lucky guy—all this and a Dodge pickup with a Hemi engine in it. Life couldn't be sweeter.*

17

A Purse Full Of Money

VICKI

Prancing out of her room, carrying her purse like it was the U.S. Mint, Katelyn was heading out the door to kindergarten, when she turned to her little sister and said, "It sure feels good to have a purse full of money."

Their mother chuckled, not thinking too much about it, supposing Katelyn had found some spare change on the floor.

That afternoon, when Sammy and I picked Katelyn up after school, we noticed a glowing smile and a spring in her step, which she usually didn't have after a long day of reading, writing, and arithmetic. She was beaming as she showed off the plastic ring proudly displayed on her finger. To her, it was the most beautiful thing she had ever seen.

Reaching over the back of Sammy's seat, she handed him a dollar bill. She exclaimed, "Here is some money, Pop-Pop. Go buy whatever you want with it."

Then she proceeded to do the same to me. When she opened her purse, we hadn't seen anything unusual. When she went to zip it back up, we noticed her purse was full of dollar bills.

When Stefani, her mother, came to pick the kids up after work, we had to share our discovery, as much as we would have liked to keep it a secret between the three of us.

Her mother asked for her purse, and you can imagine her surprise when she found fifty-two one dollar bills stuffed inside. On further questioning, the truth soon came to light. My granddaughter innocently shared, "I found the money in the pocket of Bubba's game chair."

Her brother, Austin, who was walking by, stopped dead in his tracks when he heard her explanation. "Hey, that is my birthday money. I was saving it for a new video game!"

She looked at him, reasoning in her young mind, "Since I was the one to find it, it now belongs to me!"

As they bantered back and forth, the story began to unfold. She had found the money in her brother's game chair pocket and tucked it safely away in her purse. At school, she shared two dollars with each of her friends, telling them to spend it any way they wanted. Her little eyes shined with glee as she went on about how popular she now was, and it was clear she had been Queen for a Day! She then purchased the treasured ring from one of her friends for two of the many dollars. Luckily, she had only spent twelve of the sixty-four dollars of Austin's savings.

Of course, being the typical big brother, he grabbed her arm behind her back and demanded his money back, and she grabbed the bills neatly stacked on the counter and yelled, "Finders keepers; losers weepers!"

Their mother stepped in before the situation went from bad to worse, explaining to her daughter the saying wasn't true in the real world. My granddaughter placed her hands on her little hips and with great pride retorted, "Well, it sure felt good to share! Isn't that the first thing you ever taught me to do?"

All of us (except Austin) cracked up, hiding the laughter behind our hands as Stefani jumped in to referee the struggle between finder and keeper. I had to leave the room as not to undermine her authority. As I did, I could hear mother lecturing daughter about the rules of taking things that weren't rightfully hers, how dangerous it was to carry that much money around, and all the things a mother has to say to her young daughter at times like this to teach her the ways of the world.

But being the grandma, my mind could envelope the first awakenings of womanhood—and how good she felt to have a purse full of money—and the joy she must have felt sharing it with her friends—and being the most popular kid in school for a day.

And having served my time, I was now free to just laugh and laugh and laugh.

18

What, Me Worry?

VICKI

I have seen that look before, I thought as Stefani sat at the table and yawned repeatedly. She had stopped by my house to pick up Kylie after a sleepover with MiMi. As my youngest granddaugher watched her mama yawn yet again, she crawled up in her lap and put her face in her hands.

"Mommy, how in the world do you ever sleep when I am not at home?" she asked, and I suppressed a giggle.

That night as I laughed again at her question, my mind wandered back in time to the first of many sleepless nights my children had given me.

My daughter begs me for days to go on a date—all alone—with a boy—in a car. I tell her repeatedly, "Not yet. *I* am not old enough."

So, of course, three days later, as she climbs in beside the boy in his red Pontiac Fiero—which is capable of going up to 120 miles an hour in two minutes—I make her promise she will be home by ten and not one minute after. She even pinky-swears.

So now it is one minute after ten. She isn't home, and I am frantic. The moments tick away like years, and at four minutes after, I am looking up phone numbers for the hospital—no make that the morgue—I make a mental note to add these numbers to my speed dial.

Now it is five after ten, and I am thinking, *Oh, my God, she is probably lying on the side of the road calling out, 'Mama, Mama!' and I don't know where to find her. If she does get home safely, she is never going out on a date—with a boy—in a car—again!*

It is now ten after the hour, and it is time to call the Missing Children Hotline. *Where is that magnet we got at the PTA meeting?* Another number to add to my speed dial.

"Hello," says the lady manning the hotline.

"My daughter is missing," I report.

"How long has she been missing?"

"Ten minutes . . . ." I answer.

*Click. . .*well, of all the nerve!

I can't take this anymore. My heart is pounding out of my chest, nausea envelopes my midsection, and I think I am about to faint.

It is now fifteen after the hour, and I go out on the front porch for some fresh air. Well, really to watch for headlights down our road, but I digress. I open the door—and there she is—laughing and joking with her date on the front porch swing.

"Hi, Mom, what is wrong?" she asks as she sees the panic in my face, which I am sure has aged considerably in the fifteen minutes she made me worry.

"Why didn't you let me know you were home?" I question with a voice that sounds just a little like someone who is a resident in *One Flew Over the Cuckoo's Nest*.

"Why, Mommy Dearest, we have been home twenty minutes, and it is so nice outside. We are just enjoying the full moon and conversation. Would you please close the door so I can say good night to my date?" she asks, trying not to giggle until I am back in the house and out of earshot.

I close the door, still standing on the porch.

"Mother, please!"

I reluctantly go back into the house. When she hasn't come in after five more minutes, I do what any responsible mother would do—I start blinking the lights on and off.

I hear, "Mom!" so I flip the switch to off and run to the bedroom just as she comes in and slams the door.

"Why do you embarrass me every chance you get?" she screams loud enough to wake the dead.

I reply with a smile, "It is my God-given calling."

To this day, I don't think I have ever seen anyone's eyes roll so far back in her head.

Soon everyone is in bed, and as I peek in on both kids, I thank God that again all is right with my world. They are sound asleep, looking more like my little angels than strangers who want to go out on car dates. Soon, I am peacefully dreaming of yesterdays when the only worry I had when I looked in on them was whether they were fed and dry.

But that was yesterday and yesterday's gone. Now, the kids don't live here anymore, and ever since that first umbilical cord was cut, I have had many sleepless nights. We leave the kitchen light burning like the eternal flame to let them know "The light is always on and waiting for you."

The only time the light goes off, and I sleep soundly, is when my son comes in from California, my daughter and her family sleep over, and I quietly gaze down on their sleeping faces.

Then, just like that, the moment is gone, and so are they—leaving my imagination to run wild when they don't call as often as I think they should.

No, your mother doesn't know it yet, my little grandgirl, but the answer to your innocent question, "How in the world do you ever sleep when I am not home?" lies in the hearts of all the moms whose children are no longer sound asleep, snuggled tight in their beds in their mama's house. It is a loud resounding answer, breaking the silence of the night in unison, "*We don't!*"

19

A Thing Of Beauty

SAMMY

"I need to mow the yard. Look at all of the yellow flowers growing in it," I told Vicki. Hearing my words, four-year-old Kylie, pleaded, "No, no, Pop-Pop; please don't mow down the flowers. They are so beautiful!"

I told her she could pick some for herself, but the rest had to go. I fired up my riding mower, got on, and began mowing. I looked at the flowers, and they were kind of pretty, all yellow with a pink buttercup growing here and there.

It's funny, I thought, *these flowers are a nuisance to me, but to my little granddaughter, they are beautiful. I guess it is just how you look at things.*

Kylie's view of things got me looking around our place. Our house is still nice enough, I guess. Like me, it is beginning to show signs of age. It certainly doesn't compare to some of the houses I saw n the big city the other day. You talk about some nice places, they had them. There was every design imaginable, big rambling two-story houses with multi-stone exteriors, upstairs balconies, and right on the lake. *Sweet.*

As I continued mowing, I recalled when we got this house. Wasn't it right over there by that tree Vicki and I stood admiring the brand new house we had just purchased? We were so proud, but I think each of us was secretly concerned about paying for it.

Oh, there's the rose bush I planted. It was right about that spot Stefani practiced her cheerleader routines when she made the junior high squad. I can still hear her saying, "Watch this, Daddy! *DADDY!* Watch me!"

Right there beside the house is where she and her best friend played in the mud before the yard had a blade of grass in it. They were supposed to just wade around in it, but before long, they were covered from head to toe in blackland mud. They were down and dirty, but happy. That is, until I almost froze them when I rinsed them off with cold water from the hose before I would let them even go in the garage.

I mowed along until I was under the hackberry trees in front of the house, and when I looked up, I saw one board nailed to a limb. It was the last remnant of a tree house my son and our neighbor girl constructed when they were around nine or ten years old. They were so proud. You would have thought they had built the Taj Mahal. They never knew it, but later I climbed up and put a few more nails in it to make it safer and stronger. I should remove that board, but for some reason I never have.

As I moved around back, I saw the basketball goal that Jeff and his friends spent countless hours shooting baskets and good-naturedly trash-talking each other. The backboard was getting rough, and the goal didn't even have a net. I'd wanted to take it down, but I'm glad I didn't.

He came in from California for Mother's Day, and my grandson, Austin, and he played a little one-on-one on that same old goal.

I looked down in the pasture and saw the little pond where Austin caught his first fish. I have a picture of him proudly holding up the four-inch perch for all the world to see.

Right next door is the neighbor's pasture where every day I used to take Katelyn to see their white baby donkey—I could never convince her it wasn't a goat. Each day as soon as she got here, she would ask me to take her to see the goat. I finally gave up trying to change her mind and nicknamed the donkey Billy.

I finished mowing and began weed-eating around the old swing set that has survived all three of my grandchildren. I need to haul it off, but haven't gotten around to it. I'll probably get rid of it next year or maybe the year after that. No more than three years for sure.

Hey, there's the sandbox I built for Kylie. Not the best sandbox in the world, but it served the purpose. It was just the other day she caught a butterfly that landed on it. She held it a minute and then let it go free to find its mommy.

Finally, I finished with the yard work and stood back to check out my handiwork. As I stood there looking around, I realized this house may not have all the amenities of the houses in the big city, but it does have something they don't. It has memories—my memories—*our* memories. And that makes it beautiful—especially with that patch of yellow flowers I left standing just for Kylie.

20

No More Kidding

VICKI

Sitting on the front porch every morning waiting on the kids to get out of the car and run to give me a hug was something I grew to expect and love. Every morning the same routine: Katelyn ran over and gave me a squeeze, Austin patted me on the back, and Kylie crawled up in my lap and said, "I love you, MiMi, so, so much."

I had it in my mind this time would last forever. Monday morning came, and I sleepily got out of bed, threw on my t-shirt and capris, brushed my teeth, poured me a cup of coffee and headed to the bench on the front porch, humming away.

But this morning something wasn't quite right, and as I stopped in mid-sit, reality slapped my heart. The car wouldn't be pulling up this morning, the kids wouldn't be getting out, no one would be running over, no one would be patting me on the back, and no one would be crawling up in my lap. Tears began to flow as I wondered where in the world the time had gone.

For the first time in thirty-six years, there would be no children in this house. My baby grandchild was the last. With the others, including my own children, I had felt a sense of loss as each one went off to school for the first time, but another one was always here to take his or her place. Not this time.

I could no longer sit on the front porch and watch nothing happening. *I will go inside, prop my feet up and read the paper,* I thought. *Maybe this isn't going to be so bad,* I reasoned, but the silence was way too loud. Okay, I smiled, *I can watch whatever I want on the television,* but the sight of SpongeBob as I changed the channels only brought me back to tears.

I got in the shower and tried to sing something upbeat, but the only songs I knew anymore reminded me of the kids.

I walked to the car, moved the bicycle—and skateboard—and a couple of Barbie dolls out of the way. *Work should take my mind off this nightmare,* I thought. I could catch up on some paperwork. Yes, keeping busy was the answer. As I unlocked the front door to the office, the phone was ringing.

"MiMi?" Kylie asked.

"Yes, Sweetheart," I choked back tears.

"I just wanted to say I miss you before I go to school," her little voice trembled.

"Okay," I told my daughter as she took the telephone. "Four years old is way too young to start them to school! Bring her back here, and we will do this next year. Pre-K isn't mandatory. Besides, she has the rest of her life to learn stuff. Seriously, what can they teach her that I can't?"

That ought to do it. Stefani could just bring her back here, and we could forget all this nonsense about going to school at four-years-old. Ridiculous!

But, my daughter patiently explained for the fiftieth time that her youngest wanted to go to school, that she needed to socialize with other kids, and she didn't want her to get behind.

Humph, I thought, *like I would let her get behind,* but I didn't say anything out loud. I just told her I loved her and have a great day—and that was when I felt my heart breaking into a thousand pieces. It was final, and I was off the phone and into the bathroom where the dam broke, and I sobbed uncontrollably for what seemed forever.

This is silly, I told myself, but each time I would get control, I would see a stuffed animal or markers or glue or the hundreds of little boxes the grandgirls hid their treasures in. You name it—the memories of our wonderful life were everywhere.

I tried to tell myself it wasn't like they moved far away, but I had been through this four times before, and I knew once they started school, nothing would ever be the same. I would be replaced by Ms. Whatever Her Name is this year, and instead of, "MiMi says. . . ." it will be, "My teacher says. . . ." Not that that is a bad thing, but I just wasn't ready.

So back at home, I looked around my house and all the art supplies were neatly in their drawers, and the Barbies were put away in Tupperware boxes. I didn't even step on one Lincoln Log with my bare feet, and the laughter had gone with the wind. What I would give to hear the grandkids fighting with each other over who had the most ice cream, or yell at Austin as he chased the girls down the hall for turning off his game in mid-level.

As Sammy bent over to pick up a stray toy under his chair, he said, "Why did it bother me so for toys to be everywhere?"

"I don't know," I cried a river of regrets. "Oh, Sammy, I tried so hard not to blink!"

He walked over and hugged me, kissing me on top of my head as he had done so many times before when I really needed it. He couldn't reply for the lump in his throat was too big.

Just when I thought I couldn't stand the silence any longer, it was broken by the ringing of the phone.

"Mama, the kids want to have a sleepover with you Friday night. Can you pick them up after school? They said they wanted to stay with you every weekend!" Stefani laughed.

I was just about to commit to every weekend with tears of joy running down my cheeks when the voice of reason came from the direction of where Sammy was standing, "Well, maybe not every weekend," Sammy said, "but just this once, for starters," he winked at me.

I wiped the mascara away with the palm of my hand as Sammy asked, "Want to run see what is on at the movies and get a bite to eat?"

I started to tell him there was nothing at the movies the kids could see as I had checked the paper this morning, and then I smiled. Sammy hugged me tight to his chest, and gave me a much longer kiss than usual.

Maybe this retirement thing isn't going to be half-bad after all, I thought as I grabbed my purse—as long as I got my MiMi fix more often than not.

21

Sweetest Words Ever Spoken

VICKI

Remembering the night Jeff and his Blue Devil football team played in ten-degree weather, I had flashbacks of spending the night shivering in my flannel underwear, ski pants, and Alaskan parka. The snow was coming down in giant flakes, and my feet froze to the metal stands. Several of the parents headed to the warmth of their cars. I thought, *That would feel so good.* Looking around, only a few parents were left in the freezing cold, and Sammy and I were among them.

Were we crazy? All it took to answer that question was to see my son looking up in the stands to see if we were still there. If the team could stay and play, by golly, we could stay and watch.

Out of the blue, the winds picked up, and we found ourselves in the midst of a blizzard. I must admit, when they decided to let the clock run without stopping in order to hasten the end of the game, I was more than thrilled. The sound of that final whistle was one of the sweetest sounds I had ever heard.

When Jeff took off his helmet for the last time in 1993, I said a little prayer of thanks to heaven that I would never again have to sit out in the cold rain or snow to watch one of my children play ball.

Little did I know that I would blink my eyes, and just like that, I would have grandchildren playing soccer.

Oh, yes, I secretly prayed for rain when I found out my Kylie's soccer game was at 8 o'clock on a Saturday morning, and rain it did. But much to my surprise, no one called off the games.

What? Did they *not* realize it was flu season? Geez!

But like good grandparents, we got up out of our perfectly warm bed, grabbed ponchos, loaded our lawn chairs and umbrellas, and headed for the soccer field. Before I left, the rain had stopped, and a bit of sun was peeking through the clouds. So, of course, I wore my high-heeled sandals and Capris. *After all, I didn't have to look like a grandmother!*

It seemed perfectly sensible to me that the sun would continue to shine, and it would be hot and steamy. *Not!*

We arrived at the game to find the path to the field covered in water which we had to wade through, and me in my open-toed sandals. To make matters worse, the rains started again and drenched my white capris even though I had thrown the poncho over my shoulders.

Sammy saw our son-in-law struggling to put up a tarp, so he ran ahead to help him.

I walked over to my daughter, who laughed and said, "We had a fight over bringing the tarp. I didn't want to."

"Well, my sweet daughter, this is one time I definitely agree with the son-in-law," I said.

"Write that one down on the calendar!" he quipped, winking.

Now mind you, it wasn't a very large tent, and all the parents and team huddled under it. My feet were freezing, and my wet clothes added to the chill. My teeth chattered so loud I didn't hear the opening whistle. I wasn't too worried because I was sure they would tell us all to go home any second. These were five-year-olds, for goodness sake.

So, imagine my surprise when the coach called the team out onto the field. Imagine his surprise when not one of the little girls volunteered to go.

"Well, if no one will play, we'll all just have to go home!" I yelled at the coach, hoping to help him make up his mind to call off this madness. I yelped as I got a hard poke in the ribs from Stefani.

All of a sudden, Kylie jumped up and ran out onto the field, ready to take one for her team. Two more children followed behind her, but the others refused to leave the comfort of their mother's laps.

One mother reminded her daughter, "You said it would be fun to play in the rain."

"I lied," her daughter retorted, and we all stifled our giggles. Her mother saw no humor in it, and pushed her out on the field. (After all, she was the coach's wife, and how would it look if her daughter refused to play.)

Folding her arms and sticking out her lower lip, the little blonde-haired girl stood in the middle of the field for the kick-off, and that is where she stayed. The kids played the game all around her. The referee nudged her toward the ball, but she dug her heels into her muddy chosen spot and refused to move.

We all laughed because the determination on her face clearly told her parents, *You can make me come out here on this field in the rain, but you can't make me play.*

Needless to say, she watched most of the game from underneath the tarp.

Several plays later, a sandy-haired boy on the other team was called to enter the game once again. He walked to the mid-field line, put his hands on his hips, pointed his finger at his mother and stated, "Okay, but this is absolutely the last time!"

Another of the little ones hesitated when it was her time to go in. "I'll buy you some ice cream," her mother bribed. As cold as it was, it worked. She ran out onto the field, ready to do battle for that Brahm's Birthday Cake Double Dip Waffle Cone.

On the other hand, Kylie was having a blast out there mixing it up with the other team. The coach asked her if she was ready to come out for a while. She gave him a scowl which clearly told him, *Do I look like I am ready to come out?* Then she lined up to kick the ball.

I was shaking from the cold—or was it from the pure absurdity of playing five-year-olds at 8 o'clock in the morning, in the mud, in the rain.

All of a sudden, I stopped dead in my thoughts. *Well, you really are becoming an old fuddy-duddy, aren't you?* I chided myself, smiling as I heard laughter drift through the air. My granddaughter slid into the goal following the ball—right into a mud puddle—loving every second of it.

The referee blew the whistle and yelled, "Game over!" Sammy whooped, "Sweeter words were never spoken."

All the parents said in unison, "*Amen!*"

All I could see was mud as my tomboy ran up to us and asked, "Are we going somewhere to eat?"

We all laughed, me standing there in my wet sandals, mascara running down my cheeks, and she dripping mud from one end to the other.

But for some odd reason, I heard, "Sure!" come out of my mouth. I stood there trying to figure out why, amidst her shouts of glee.

Sammy, on the other hand, looked at me and asked, "Have you lost your ever-loving mind?"

I smiled, and hand-in-hand we walked to the car. As I opened the back door, I thanked God for leather seats. Hoisting her into her car seat, she hugged me, mud and all. "I love you, MiMi. Thank you for coming to my game."

I beamed at Sammy because I knew *those* were really the sweetest words that had ever been spoken.

"Wouldn't have missed it for the world," I fudged.

Sammy rolled his eyes, snickered, not believing his always not-a-hair-out-of-place, makeup perfect, permanent-pressed little wife was going anywhere looking like a drowned rat—and she was doing it with a smile on her face. He shook his head, chuckled, and as he looked in the rear view mirror, all he could see were the whites of Kylie's sparkling eyes and the brightest smile ever flashed, and he almost understood—almost.

22

Austin

SAMMY

*A*few years ago—well, it was more like several years ago—okay, it was 1995—our daughter was the girl's track coach for dear old Celeste High School. And that very year, she was fortunate to have a team of girls qualify to run the mile relay in the state track meet.

Now as it happened, she was expecting her first child. Knowing it was to be a boy, the girls on the team suggested he be named Austin, after the town in which they were running, to commemorate their competing in the state meet there.

"You know, that's not a bad idea. What do you think, Dad?" Stefani asked.

"I just thank God the state meet wasn't held in Pflugerville," I replied.

So later that year, my first grandchild was born. Right from the get-go we could tell Austin didn't take after my wife, Vicki, or me— *he was a quiet child.* He hardly ever cried and was quite content to play alone. Even though he couldn't read, he would amuse himself by taking children's books and going over every letter, word, number or picture on every page of every book.

He continued with his quiet ways throughout childhood and even into his early teen years. He would talk to you, though, ask questions, and even joke around some.

But that was yesterday and yesterday's gone. He's seventeen now. You know, the age when it's hard to even be around old folks, much less talk to them.

Hey, do you think that deters us? No way. He's got the wrong grandparents to get away with that.

"How are you doing, son?" Vicki asked.

"Umm," Austin mumbled while looking at his phone.

"School going okay?" I wondered.

"Mmmmnh," he grunted.

"Still playing the guitar?" we inquired.

"Yeah," he replied.

"O-M-G!" Vicki and I exclaimed in unison as we gleefully hugged each other. "He said a word! We have broken the conversation age barrier!"

As excited as if we were reliving the moment when he said his first word as a baby, we blurted out, "We love you, Grandson! Thanks for talking to us!"

"Okay. Yeah. Whatever," he said as he headed up to his room.

Three words this time! No, it wasn't a sentence, but we were excited. We had accomplished something few people our age have done in recent history. We had conversed with a teenager face-to-face!

A couple of weeks later, we had Austin alone in our car as we gave him a ride home. Vicki, remembering the three words he pieced together awhile back, was encouraged to try to engage him in more conversation.

"Why don't you tell us about what is going on in your life?" she asked.

"Actually, I'm not all that interesting," he replied.

"Let me ask you this," she continued, not giving up. "What do you think about us?"

"Well, I guess you are okay, but sometimes it's really hard to understand what you are talking about," he confessed. "And to be honest, I think you are pretty old. I mean, I can't ever see myself looking as old as y'all do."

Talk, talk, talk, I thought, *My gosh, can't that kid ever shut up?*

23

I Can Quit Anytime I Want To

VICKI

"The ball did *not* touch her! You need to get glasses!" Katelyn, yelled to the referee during her six-year-old sister, Kylie's basketball game.

"Katie, settle down, you are embarrassing us! You sound just like MiMi," Austin, laughed—half-joking, half-serious.

For a second, I was taken aback. Was I really that bad?

I had tried and tried to quit. Every time I yelled at the referees, I swore it would never happen again—I could quit anytime I wanted to—I could! But the truth is, if I were being honest, I'd be found guilty. They say the first step in solving a problem is admitting you have one—so there—I said it—sort of.

It all started when my daughter began playing basketball in third grade. At first it was little jibes from me, "Hey, Ref, are you blind?"

Then I went a little further, "Ref, when was the last time you took an eye test? You can't even see a travel?"

I knew I was really out of control the night I yelled, "Hey, Ref, who'd you get your glasses from, Stevie Wonder?" and Sammy just hid his face in his hands and cried.

I tried to quit. Before each game, I would give myself a pep talk:

Listen, Vicki, you have to remain calm. Have you noticed your friends sit three seats down from you, your husband is afraid you are going to have a heart attack, and your son tells everyone you haven't been taking your medication?

It got so bad, one friend on my son's basketball team told me they had to watch the films of the game with the volume turned down because I yelled so loud.

And then one day, just like magic, I stopped yelling. I was cured!

Of course, my children had played their last games, and I no longer was as passionate about other people's children getting bad calls. But hey, I didn't yell at one referee for all those years.

Then, I fell off the wagon. My little girl had grown up and started coaching her little girl's first grade basketball team. I told myself:

You are okay. You have matured in the last fifteen years. You were just a kid back then. Now you are someone's grandmother, and you have to set a good example.

I felt confident as I took my seat in the stands. The clock counted down to the start of the game—I was good—I was smiling, because I knew how proud my family was going to be of me. Then the whistle blew.

A giant of a first grader came out of nowhere and stole the ball from little Kylie, causing her to trip and fall. The referee just ran down court and watched this—this—half-grown girl put the ball into the basket without calling a foul. Before I knew what was happening, I heard a woman yelling, "Ref, didn't you see that? What do you wash your contacts with, Milk of Magnesia?"

Sammy pulled me back into my seat. I realized the woman was me, and Austin had scooted to the other side of the bleachers. "Okay, no more! I am just going to sit here and watch the game. I won't say one word," I promised Sammy. I was really proud of myself. I had gotten it out of my system. I experienced a few setbacks, with an occasional, "She is on her back!" or "Three seconds, Ref?" but nothing to send me to rehab over or anything.

Out of nowhere, the mean-green-fighting machine, who had gotten away with more murder that night than Freddy Kruger, plowed into little Kylie again sending her sprawling into the back wall.

In disbelief, I saw the ref raise his hand to the back of his head and yell, "Charging!" on my little angel.

I heard a woman yell, "This is *not* a contact sport! If she is hurt, we will be sending you the bill!"

I looked at Sammy, and he wasn't looking back at me scowling, so I was pretty sure it wasn't me—but, *they* had drawn first blood—and the shark that lives inside me was circling the prey. Before I could stop it, it went in for the kill, "Yes, and you can afford it because you certainly aren't spending any money on glasses!"

I looked down to see if I was going to get a high-five from the mom of Kylie's teammate who had yelled first and realized the screamer had been my daughter—the sweet, gentle coach—who was now stomping her foot and clapping her hands at the referee—and I realized we had just tag-teamed this man.

Sammy was staring at us as if we had just degraded a poor soul who was only trying to earn a few extra dollars to put braces on his child's teeth, instead of this monster that was picking on my innocent, precious grandbaby. He mouthed, "Like mother, like daughter?"

I gave him my best apologetic smile, and he thought I was feeling guilty. But deep down, I was proud of my daughter for taking up for our little girl and having a passion about her that lends to speaking her mind.

I sat down, and Sammy thought I had learned my lesson, but when I saw he wasn't looking, I gave my daughter a thumbs-up.

In the distance, I listened. I could hear other mothers and fathers yelling, "She is living in the lane!"

The lady beside me yelled, "One more call like that, and I am unfriending you on Facebook!"

Everyone laughed, and I wished I had thought of it. I smiled and looked at Sammy and Austin.

This time it wasn't me. Maybe I should start a support group. I think I'll call it, "Yell-a-non."

24

I Feel Your Pain

SAMMY

*S*he sat silently as she watched the children laughing and play-ing on the playground equipment at the restaurant. I observed her as her eyes followed each move the youngsters made as they ran, climbed, and went up and down the slide. After a few minutes, I asked, "Why aren't you joining in the fun, Kylie?"

"Because I'm too old," my granddaughter lamented, "which is ridiculous!" she continued, sounding mature beyond her years. "My gosh, I'm only nine-years old. But if I go over there, they won't play with me and will probably make fun of me, too." She became quiet again and looked somewhat dejected as she picked at her food.

Oh no! You, too? I thought. Could it be true? More than a half-century separated our ages, yet we both were experiencing some of the same feelings concerning getting older? I really figured Kylie had about forty-five or fifty years before the age thing reared its ugly head.

"Welcome to my world, Kylie. I feel your pain," I sighed. "The fact is you'll probably have to stick with people closer to your age to be accepted. That's just the way it is."

Now you know I'm just kidding about Kylie being shunned due to her age. What she was feeling was just the way kids treat one another.

But, me? Eh, I'm not so sure. In the last few years it seems there is a marked difference in the way people treat me. The signs are subtle at first—little things such as the rolling of their eyes when I start talking—no wait—strike that—folks have been doing that to me since I was a teenager.

However, I do notice other things to indicate younger folks want to avoid me—like leaving the room when I enter—or picking a table as far away from me as possible—or suddenly doing an about face and walking the other way when they see me coming. Actually, the walking away doesn't bother me all that much. It is when they start running that hurts a little.

Then there is the huddle. You haven't seen this one? That's when a group of less age-challenged people is standing around enjoying interacting with one another. They see Methuselah headed their way. Immediately, they huddle up with arms around each other, backs toward the possible intruder. They don't do this to be disrespectful, but more to help each other refrain from engaging the ancient one in conversation which could inadvertently lead to one of them asking him this question, "How are you doing?"

Because if that happens, my goodness, they know they will be there for a while.

The Elder will begin by telling them about his current physical condition. Then, he will segue into his medical history, complete with naming each ailment, doctors, dates of treatments, hospitals, and how that one place had the cutest little nurse you ever did see.

Next up is his work history, military service, and political views. They pretend to listen and begin to make excuses to leave, but he won't stop. He goes on and on. By now, they are all praying one of those drones they have heard so much about will either take him— or them—out.

Finally, one of the younger ladies comes up with an idea. She shouts that it is almost time for *Wheel of Fortune*. When the senior hears that, he stops talking and sprints to his car, trying to get to a TV before Vanna is introduced.

As you can see, it's not all on the juniors. We seniors could do a little better at not making it all about us. We should remember, or give it our best shot at remembering—we were young once and felt the same way about the generation above us. We have to acknowledge some of their ideas might be better, and they should do the same for us.

Yeah, we may be different ages, and we might not have the same views on some things. When you get right down to it, those things don't really matter. The fact is we are all in the same boat now. And it sure seems like we are heading for one humongous waterfall with swirling rapids below. We need to change direction. And to do that, we have to all be paddling together.

Let's do it for each other. . .and *old* Kylie.

25

Elderly? Wash Your Mouth Out

VICKI

"Someone in my class asked if the ladies who came to teach us about school history were elderly," Kylie informed me as she got in the car after school the other day.

"What did you say?" I laughed, knowing that one of those ladies was me.

"I let them know right quick my grandmother was not elderly," Kylie replied.

"Why do you think they asked that?" I asked her.

"Maybe because you called a refrigerator an icebox," she shrugged.

Whew! Scared me for a minute—I thought it might have been how I looked!

Elderly? My mind couldn't grasp the notion that anyone would think that I was elderly. That is such a dirty word. Anyone saying it needs to have his/her mouth washed out with soap. Why, I am the poster child for the fountain of youth! Aren't I? Well, maybe not in the eyes of eight-year-olds.

Little did I know while I was teaching them history, they thought my life was just about over. I should have gotten the hint when one of the little boys asked me if I was alive when Celeste was discovered.

I admit when I look in the mirror, I don't recognize this gray-haired woman looking back at me. And when people comment, "You haven't changed a bit since high school," I want to scream, "Please, God, tell me I didn't look like this in high school!"

And I can tell you right now, I agree with the old adage, "Wrinkled is not one of the things I wanted to be when I grew up!"

Lately conversations with people my age have become more a contest of what ails us. At the 60s reunion, I had to laugh as I watched the men comparing their heart surgery scars, men just a tad older than I. These friends are the same ones who lived life in the fast lane. One of them quipped, "Now I am being warned to slow down—by my doctor—not the highway patrol."

So what if I don't look the same as I did eons ago, nor does my body move as fast as it once did? And what if lying about my age is so much easier now because I can't remember what it is half the time?

The truth is, it isn't how many times the hour hand has gone around on my ticking clock that makes me feel older, but how the world starts to make me feel.

Those who know me know I have never been one to conform to the ways of this world. One of my friends told me the other day, "You are the kind of person who will die young—at a ripe old age." Gotta love a friend like that!

I refuse to let the status quo get inside my head! And for your information, inside my head is a pretty, young kiddo screaming, "I am still young, vibrant, alive and kicking in here." I can tell you that right now!

I think I will take my friend up on her advice and throw out all nonessential numbers—starting with age, weight and height. How old would I be if I didn't know how old I was? Way younger than what it says on my driver's license, I can guarantee you that!

So I have decided to only run around with people at least twenty years older than I am (if I can still find any). They all think I am still a young'un! And when I get their age, I pledge to remember how young they really were.

But my mama didn't raise no fool! I am wise enough to decide when I want to be young, and when I want to be. . . well. . .seasoned, because I still might need to play my longevity card for things like getting into the ballgames free, or twenty-percent off meals, or discount shopping days at my favorite dress shop (although I am sure everyone will think I have faked my ID just to get the savings.)

But, elderly—not in my lifetime!

26

Rotflmho

VICKI

"Austin, look at me and stop texting for a second," my daughter told her thirteen-year-old son.

"Just a second," he replied, but five minutes later his thumbs were still flying across the keyboard. Rather intrigued, I wondered how he could type out messages that fast with just two digits. Stefani, on the other hand, found no fascination in his talent whatsoever.

She warned him, "Tell your friend it is too late to text someone and ask him not to text here again tonight. Your grandparents have come to visit, and we are trying to have some family time. If you text after that, you will be grounded from the phone for two days, and I mean it!"

Austin mumbled under his breath, but sent the message. He put his phone in his pocket, sensing from the tone of his mother's voice that she would, indeed, submit to such torture as sending him out into the world without a cell phone if he didn't comply with her demands.

No sooner had we started to play a game, when we heard the now-too-familiar ping, telling him someone had messaged him back.

As I watched the battle of the wills over whether Austin would get to answer the text, or his mother would rule the roost, it seemed as if it was just a blink ago when Stefani was thirteen, and a similar scenario started playing in my mind:

1985

The phone rings for the twelfth time tonight, and I feel a scream rising in my throat. I try to picture what my thirteen-year-old daughter looked like without a receiver as part of her anatomy. Too weary to get up and tell her to get off the phone again, I have a moment of temporary insanity as I ask her nine-year-old brother to go and tell her to hang up.

Jeff picks up the extension and screams into the receiver, "Mama said hang up, *now!*"

That was definitely *not* the smartest move he ever undertook. A raging bull would have been a more welcome sight than the snarling, nostril-flaring adolescent charging after her brother. Just when I fear she will wring his neck before I can prevent his demise, my daughter stops in mid-choke and locks eyes with me. She repeats the only nine words she has spoken to me in several days, "I have never been so humiliated in all my life," then the phone rings, and Jeff is saved by the bell.

"I'll get it," she yells. Followed by, "Just a minute, I have to change phones. Mom, please hang up when I pick up in my room, and I *mean* it!"

After about thirty minutes of giggling and whispering, I get up and open her door to give her my well-rehearsed lecture, "You are lucky, young lady, I let you talk as long as I have. When I was a kid, we had a five-minute time limit."

Just as I am finishing with ". . . you know your father didn't even have a phone when he was growing up," she hangs up.

"It is all right, Mom. My friend understands. Her parents were giving her the same sermon. You all sound like a broken record. Excuse me, I think I am going to be violently ill," she says as she slams the door behind me.

"Listen to me, Miss Astor, one more word like that out of you, and you will be grounded from the phone for life!"

*T*he sound of a ringtone in the distance brought me back to the present. Exasperated, Stefani put down the die, told Austin to answer the phone, and inform whoever it was to cease and desist calling for the night.

"Then turn the phone off, Austin!" she yelled after him.

Talking softly for about thirty seconds, Austin hung up, turned the phone off, and rejoined us in our game of Sour Apples to Apples.

"See there, Austin, that wasn't so hard, now was it?" Stefani asked.

His eyes gleaming, Austin answered, "Not at all. The phone call was for *you*. She called my phone since yours was off, but I told her it was way too late to be receiving calls and to please not call or text for the rest of the night as we were trying to have family time, just as you told me."

I tried not to. I really did. I even turned my head so they couldn't see that I was ROTFLMHO—oh, yea, that is text speak for "Rolling on the floor laughing my head off."

27

Bed, Bath And Beyond

VICKI

"What I would give for a hot bath and a little alone time before bed—sometimes I think I will be glad when my kids grow up," Stefani sighed.

I chuckled out loud. Yes, I recall feeling that way once upon a time myself.

Several years ago, I was feeling exceptionally stressed after a rough day of motherhood, so I thought I would take a long, hot, sudsy bath. Remembering some expensive shower gel I had received as a gift many Christmases back—but hadn't had time or opportunity to use—I opened the lid. When I went to pour it into the tub, I realized it was so old, it smelled more like toilet bowl cleaner than a luxurious perfume. The hardened glob wouldn't budge out of the bottle.

My eyes fell on my young son's bottle of He-Man Bubble Bath sitting on the ledge. I sighed and resigned myself that it would have to do.

Before I could actually fill the tub with glorious suds, I had to spend five minutes of my self-promised hour cleaning it out. After removing the toy wrestlers, Barbies, GI Joes, My Little Ponies, and a Freaky Freddy Mad Ball, I got excited as I saw the steaming water fill the tub with bubbles. Ah, the smell of Bubble Gum! Not exactly the fragrance I had hoped for, but I was still happy to lower myself into the soothing water.

I turned on the whirlpool bath attachment—the first time it had been out of the box.

Wow! I thought as I immersed myself into the hot swirling spa. I sighed with contentment, *Ah, where have you been for the last ten years? So this is where Calgon takes you away to.*

A knock shattered my peace. Before I could say, "Don't come in," my ten-year-old daughter marched to my side, her face red with anger.

"Mama! You have got to do something with your son. I have homework to do, and he is bouncing all over the bed!"

I raised both hands as if to say, *What in the world do you expect me to do about it right now?*

Unexpectedly, the look on my face brought a smile to hers. She said, "Oh, yeah, guess I'll tell Dad. Mama, you have a nice bath!" as she backed out of the room.

Immediately forgetting the interruption, I drifted back into the land of contentment—then another knock at the door. "I have to get up early. I am headed to bed. If you don't mind, Stef needs someone to keep Jeff out of her room so she can finish her homework," my husband, Sammy, suggested. "Oh, yeah, I love ya. Go ahead and finish your bath first."

Determined I was going to finish this bath if it was the last thing I ever did, I belittled myself for not locking that darn door.

Straining to see if I could hear more chaos, I waited a bit before I got back to my happy place. Finally, all seemed quiet on the home front, so I picked up my razor and was shaving the frothy lather off my leg when my son burst through the door—this time, no knock—and thought it would be hilarious to throw a large rubber spider into the tub!

I screamed, not so much at the spider, but at the huge hunk of skin I had just cut out of my leg. The whirlpool immediately sucked up the spider and spat it out into a thousand pieces. As I sat in the midst of the assorted, misplaced body parts of the spider—the bubbles turning red from the blood pouring out of my wound—my Calgon moment now seemed more like a Stephen King horror story. The sight sent my son running from the room like a speeding bullet.

I gave up and rose from the tub. As I toweled the ruddy froth from my body, I heard Sammy soothing a distraught Jeff. I didn't know if he was more upset because he had ruined my bath, he had seen the water turn red, or he had lost his favorite rubber spider.

I had to laugh when I heard Stefani warning Sammy and Jeff, "Dad, you better take him over to Grandma's house until she calms down. Jeff, it has finally happened—Mom is going to *kill* you!"

In my mind's eye, I could see her mischievous smirk as she got the desired result. Jeff screamed louder, and Sammy sent Stefani to her room. I reluctantly pulled on my flannel nightgown and headed out of my fantasy and into the land of family to try to put out all the fires.

*Y*es, on more than one night, chaos reigned in our house. I can laugh about it now, though the humor was lost on me at the time.

Today, I can run a clean tub of hot water (no toys to remove) pour in fancy bath bubbles (which smell like perfume, not bubble gum) slip into the tub until the water turns cold every day of the week, and no one runs in to disturb me.

But young mothers—as stressful as it gets—be careful what you wish for. I would trade a thousand baths for just one more night of getting out of that tub, wrapping a bandage around my leg, sitting down with my little girl to help her with her homework, tucking my little boy into his bed, listening to them say their prayers, and kissing them both goodnight. The love I felt seeing those little *angels* sleeping peacefully is what I miss the most.

Yes, parents, take a minute to enjoy the bedlam. Your kids will grow up—too soon.

28

My Kids Would Never Do That

VICKI

*I*t had been a long day of fun at the pool, blowing bubbles and throwing water balloons. We had enjoyed a nice dinner, and I naively thought I had the grandkids settled in to watch a movie. I leaned the recliner back, picked up my laptop to check my Facebook wall and maybe take a nap. While I was waiting for my computer to boot up, the house was cool and quiet, and I drifted off into a soft slumber. A few minutes later, I was startled awake by a loud bang coming from the bedroom.

"I was watching that. Turn it back! Give me the remote control, *now*!" Austin threatened Katelyn.

"I don't have to mind you. You are not the boss of me!" Katelyn hollered back.

I heard a smack, then chairs falling over. Before I could respond, I saw Katelyn coming down the hall lickety-split with Austin fast on her heels. She was seething, and Austin had the look of eradication on his face. I was sure if he caught her before I caught him, she would be a goner.

"What in the world is going on? I have played with you all day. Can I not have a moment of peace and quiet without you two fighting?" I addressed my grandchildren.

Katelyn hid behind my chair as Austin tried to get to her, rocking the recliner back and forth with me in it.

"Stop it, right now! Geez, my kids never acted like *this*!"

Austin stopped trying to wring Katelyn's neck for a second, "I don't mean to be disrespectful, MiMi, but that isn't what you wrote about Uncle J and Mama in her scrapbook."

"What do you mean?" I asked as he pulled the scrapbook from the bookshelf. He opened it to the newspaper article I had written, August 31, 1989.

I am on the front porch reading a book when my daughter Stefani and son Jeff's words drift through the window:

STEFANI: You wash.

JEFF: No, Mama said you have to wash.

STEFANI: Why do I always have to wash? You never have to do anything. You are the favorite. Her little *baby*! You always get your way. You make me sick!

JEFF: Where am I supposed to dump this food off the plates since you are so stupid you filled up the sink with rinse water before I had time to do it? And don't tell me I am the favorite. You always get everything you want because you are a *girl*!

STEFANI: W-h-a-t-e-v-e-r! You will just have to go to the bath-room and dump it in the commode because you goofed off so long, the sink filled up with clean water.

JEFF: Mama! Stefani won't let me rinse off the dishes!

(Sound of silence)

Mama said let me rinse off the dishes in the sink.

STEFANI: She did *not*. She didn't say a word. *Liar, Liar, pants on fire!*

JEFF: It takes one to know one! Well, I can't put this food in the commode. I will throw up.

STEFANI: Just do it! Mama, Jeff won't clean off the table!

(Sound of silence)

Mama said clean off the table.

JEFF: Did *not*! Why do I always have to rake the food off the plates? I get all the *sloppy* jobs—sloppy, get it? Slop? Oh, I am just too funny!

STEFANI: Ha, Ha! You are so funny I forgot to laugh!

(Sound of the water draining out of the sink so Jeff can rake the leftovers into the garbage disposal)

Now, get those dishes cleaned off so I can get done here. A two-minute job shouldn't take two hours. . .*Baby.*

(Slap)

What the hey? Mama, Jeff hit me!
(Slapping sound as Stefani hits Jeff back)

JEFF: If you hit me again, I will punch your face in— too late—someone already beat me to it.

(Sound of maniacal laughter)

STEFANI: Jeff, you are so *not* funny. Now get over here and do your job, *now*!

JEFF: Mama! Come whup Stefani! She just gave me a wrist rope burn, and I didn't do *anything*.

STEFANI   (through clenched teeth): You've got that right, Buddy. You haven't done a dang thing!

(Thump. . .slap. . .sound of chair overturning)

Infuriated, I get up from my bench on the porch to settle this once and for all. I enter the kitchen. Stefani makes a beeline to the sink, and Jeff quickly begins to wipe the dishes.

ME: What in the world is going on in here?

STEFANI and JEFF (in unison, angelically):
Nothing, Mama. We were just having fun cleaning the kitchen. . . like you asked us to.

*T*here it was, in black and white, evidence my kids weren't angels. Darn columns! I much more preferred my selective memory.

I started to lecture the grands that my kids really never would have acted like that, and that I had just used artistic freedom in that article, when I heard Austin tell Katelyn, "Last one to the remote is a rotten egg!" Both took off giggling and pushing each other out of the way.

I leaned back in the recliner and closed my eyes, hoping I could have at least two minutes of quiet—before the next call for help came.

29

No Way, Fontay

VICKI

"MiMi, I just have to have this Ariel Mermaid for my birth-day. It swims, and we can play with it in the pool," Katelyn begs.

"I want one, too. If we don't get them, we will just die. We need them!" Kylie adds almost in tears.

"You two don't need another Barbie, Ariel, or toy for that matter," Sammy says. He looks at me, and his eyes say, *Case closed*.

"You heard Pop-Pop," I tell them sadly, seeing the disappoint-ment on their faces. I head away from the display before World War III erupts right there in the toy aisle. I continue getting my supplies when I have a flashback of a similar situation in our lives where the roles were reversed. Their mama was turning fourteen and. . . .

"*D*addy, can I have a puppy? I just saw the cutest little Pekapoo in the paper, and it will be weaned right at my birthday?" Stefani asked six weeks before the special day.

"*No way*," Sammy exclaimed with meaning. "We are *not* having a house dog!"

"Daddy, may I please have that puppy for my birthday?" Stefani implored four weeks before the big event. "I will feed it every day and make sure it has water. It won't be any trouble to you or Mama."

"*No way!*" Sammy asserted. "Puppies chew up everything and ruin the carpet. Been there, done that."

"Daddy, all I want for my birthday is that cute little ball of fur," Stefani begged three weeks before the much awaited celebration. "I will train him to the paper and give him a bath every day."

"*No way!*" Sammy banned the notion. "Dogs make the whole house smell, and the vet bills will break us for sure."

"Daddy, I have to have that little doggie. *I need it!*" Stefani appealed two weeks before the fast approaching deadline. "I will pick up after him, train him to the paper, and shampoo the carpets every Saturday. You won't even know he is in the house."

"*No way!*" Sammy flat refused. "We are *not* getting the dog, Stefani. It isn't fair to our other dog, Old Jack, to make him stay outside while a new dog gets to stay in the house."

"Daddy, I have never wanted anything as bad in all my life as I want this puppy!" Stefani beseeched one week before her fourteenth birthday. "I'll never ask you for anything again as long as I live."

"*No way!* I am *not* going to change my mind this time, so quit asking," Sammy said, emphatically. "We don't need a puppy, and that is that. End of discussion."

The night before her birthday, Stefani looked at her daddy with those sad, large puppy dog eyes and batted her eyelashes. "Daddy, please! I just have to have that puppy! Without it, I will just curl up and die!"

Using a different psychology, she gave it one last effort. "I need something of my very own to teach me responsibility," she coerced, letting the tears flow.

He crinkled his forehead, which she knew meant, *Case closed*. As she dragged down the hall to her bedroom, she looked back every few steps to make sure he was watching.

I was actually pretty proud of my husband for standing his ground on this decision. When he raised his eyebrows over his glasses, Stefani sadly admitted defeat and slammed her door—twice.

The next morning, I was shaken from a deep slumber at the crack of dawn. Sammy was fully dressed. "What happened?" I sat up, suddenly very awake. "Where are you going at this time of morning?"

"*S-h-h-h*," he whispered. "We have to hurry to the Kennel to pick up Stefani's birthday present," he winked at me, smiling from ear to ear. And so, *No Way Fontay* came into our lives.

"*P*lease, MiMi, please buy us those Ariel swimming mermaids. We will play with them in the pool every day, and take care of them and. . . ." The grandgirls stop short when they see the affirmative smile on my face.

"Go get them," I say with a grin.

Sammy comes around the corner to see what all the squealing and laughing is about. When he sees the girls holding the dolls and jumping up and down, he huffs, crosses his arms, and gives me that look of disapproval. "I told you they didn't need another toy."

"Well, I was just remembering No Way Fontay, and how I had to clean up after that puppy, how he chewed up my favorite high heels, and ruined my brand new carpet. Payback is heck," I say with a twinkle in my eyes.

He looks at me incredulously, "That happened over twenty years ago!"

"Consider yourself lucky," I laugh. "The Ariel dolls only cost $9.99, no vet bills, and they *don't* have to be house trained."

30

Oldies But Goodies—Songs That Had Meaning

VICKI

As Katelyn and Kylie sang along with Selena Gomez on the radio, I was struck with the realization that most of the songs of today followed the 7-11 rule—seven words sang eleven times.

I could hear the three singing together and the words *miss me* and *dizzy* followed by *round and round* were repeated over and over again.

I thought about pulling out my 45s and playing them on the turntable. I fully intended to lecture them about how well songs were written in my day, and how they had *real meaning*—how they didn't just sing the same words over and over—they taught lessons about how to make the world a better place.

Then I had a flashback of a rainy afternoon in the 80s.

I am listening to my teenage daughter singing along with songs on the radio. I hated when my mother didn't like my music in the 60s, but I can't help myself. I blurt out, "Stefani, why do you listen to those songs which do nothing to make the world a better place? Most of those songs are so silly they don't make any sense at all. Come upstairs with me and listen to some songs of my day. They all had a message to the youth of how to live a cut above the rest."

Stefani follows me reluctantly. About halfway up the steps, she stops, smiles and says, "Oh, I can't wait to listen to *oldies but goodies*."

The tone she uses did nothing to convince me she will listen to my songs with an objective ear.

The closer I get to the turntable, the more excitement I feel. Stefani picks up the first record, "Look here, Mom, play this one. It sounds like it might have taught you all about non-violence in the world."

I blush as she hands me "One Eyed, One Horned Flying Purple People Eater."

"Well, let's just forget that one," I stammer and hide the record at the bottom of the stack.

"Oh, here's one, Mom! This one sounds full of innocence and modesty," she giggles. Before I can respond, she holds a vinyl record album. *Boogity Boogity.* "This ought to be good!" she says, almost rapturing.

I start to tell her, "Never mind, don't look, Stefani," but it is too late. She has already looked, and she drops the needle onto the 33 1/3 piece of plastic.

I cringe as Ray Stevens sings about a man they call The Streak running amuck—wearing nothing but a smile. I stifle a giggle or two as the fastest man on two feet comes running through the pole beans naked as a jaybird, then moons Ethel right in front of the shock absorbers, and later he gives her a free *shot* at the basketball game.

But Stefani loses all sense of composure as Ray croons for Ethel to get *her* clothes back on. My daughter is beside herself and thoroughly enjoying watching me desperately searching for one record that has a serious message as she plays *The Streak* all the way through—twice!

"Here's another one, Mother Dear. And I thought your generation wore pantaloons for beach fashion." She seems to be enjoying this way too much as she holds up "Itsy Bitsy, Teenie Weenie Yellow Polka-Dot Bikini."

I am just about to explain to her that it really is a sad tale of a young girl who really was so nervous when she wore her yellow polka-dot bikini that she would not come out of the locker. She thinks she can do it, but bless her little heart, she can't do it; so, she wraps up in a blanket and makes her way to the beach. At last, she makes it to the water, but is too shy to come out—despite the fact that she is so cold she starts to turn blue.

Yes, I was going to tell my daughter that when she informs me, "We learned in U. S. history that *this* very record came out at a time when bikini bathing suits were still seen as too risqué to be permissible. In fact, the bikini caused such a public outcry, the inventor named it after the nuclear testing at Bikini Atoll. I guess you know the Catholic Church deemed it a sin to wear one. But this song caused bikini sales to soar through the roof. It set a precedence to accept girls going around the beach wearing little clothing, much to the dismay of their parents."

She sighs, shakes her head, and gives me a look as if to ask if I really knew *anything* about the music of my generation. She picked up another record.

If there is one thing that dills my pickle, it is a smart aleck kid!

But she had moved on, "Oh, look, here is a song all about medicine. Probably why so many of your generation grew up to be doctors," she teases as "Love Potion No. Nine" fills the air. "You know some stations wouldn't play this song because he kissed a cop down at 34th and Vine, don't you?" she asks, waiting for me to give her an explanation. None is forthcoming.

"You have several more songs here with significant purpose, Mama," she says facetiously.

Why do teenagers take such joy in seeing their parents squirm?

As she reads the titles: "Rhapsody in the Rain," "Silhouettes on the Shade," and "You Can't Roller Skate in a Buffalo Herd," her laughter reaches a higher pitch with each title.

"I've had enough for one night," I concede as she skips out, waving "Hey there, Little Red Riding Hood."

*T*he words *round and round* brought me back to my grandgirls. I decided to forgo the lecture and grabbed their hands. We danced round and round the room. Their eyes widened as I did the Twist—just for a second—before I felt my back go out.

Oh, well, what do you expect from a product of the 60s?

31

Pop-Pop Won't Quit Singing

SAMMY

I like music, and I like to sing. I have always sung around the house. I won't say that my wife and kids enjoyed it—more like endured it—if the truth be told. Still, it was only natural for me to sing to my grandchildren when they came along. Often, I would sing to them in the car as I took them from place to place.

When Austin was around three years old, I picked him up from daycare. As usual I started singing, and after a little while, I heard Austin cry, "*Stop!*" I started pulling over to the side of the road.

"Why do you need to stop? Do you need to go to the restroom?" I asked.

"No," he replied, "Stop singing!"

"Why?" I asked.

"Because," he answered. "It is not good!"

Well, I thought to myself, *it's probably just the song.* After all, I couldn't expect a child his age to appreciate the beauty of a song such as "She Wore an Itsy-Bitsy, Teeny-Weeny, Yellow Polka-Dot Bikini."

Undeterred, I began singing another children's classic "Oo Ee Oo Ah Ah Ting Tang Walla Walla Bing Bang."

"No more!" Austin yelled. "No more!"

Okay. OKAY! So you are too young to appreciate lyrics about a witch doctor. I'll try something else to entertain you, I determined. He ought to enjoy this one "It Was a One-eyed, One-horned, Flying Purple People Eater."

"Quit singing! Quit singing, Pop-Pop!" Austin was begging as I pulled up to our place of business. I stopped, and as soon as I got him out of his car seat, he ran for the building and burst through the door, screaming and crying at the top of his lungs.

"What's the matter?" Stefani and Vicki inquired in unison.

"Pop-Pop's singing, and he won't stop!" Austin yelled through his tears. Vicki and Stefani recoiled in horror, obviously recalling all the years of musical torture I had put them through.

"There, there. Don't worry. He won't sing to you again," they assured him.

You got that right! I thought as I hung my head and slinked out of the agency while the customers stared, and my wife and daughter glared. *I will never sing to that little Simon Cowell again!*

But just the other day as I was taking him out to his other grand-parents' house, he and his sisters were arguing and grabbing at each other.

"Stop it!" I said. No response. "I mean it, now! *Stop it,*" I insisted, my voice rising. They ignored me, totally.

"If y'all don't stop it, I am going to start singing," I threatened. They continued unabated.

When I broke out in a stirring rendition of "When the Saints Go Marching In," they immediately stopped fighting. But I was on a roll now.

When I finally finished the song, I warned them, "I know a hun-dred songs, and if y'all can't act right, I swear I'll sing every one of them!"

They stared at me as if in shock and nodded they understood.

Ah, music. It has the power to touch one's soul. It can make you laugh, cry, sing and dance. And delivered by the right person, it can make three grandchildren behave.

32

O-M-G, I Digress

VICKI

"O-M-G, why can't the pars just chillax?" Carly, the main character from the *I Carly* cable TV show, asks as she rolls her eyes and flutters her eyelashes at her friends who are hanging on to her every word. My grandchildren and I were sitting cross-legged in my living room in front of the television, a glass of Dr. Pepper in one hand and a bowl of popcorn between us. They seemed to be having no problem with this statement whatsoever. On the other hand, I frowned, deeply confused.

"What is the matter, MiMi? Don't you like this show?" Kylie asked.

"I would if I could understand a word that was said," I replied.

Austin felt it was his duty to interpret for me, "She said, 'Oh my goodness, why can't my parents just chill and relax?'"

"Well, why can't she just speak English?" I questioned.

"Oh, MiMi, you are so yesterday!" Katelyn added. The sound of giggles filled the room. Austin was laughing so hard Dr. Pepper squirted out his nose. I watched them in amusement until the laughter died down, and they wiped the happy tears from their eyes.

"Yesterday? I'll show you yesterday! I remember when we had our own lingo back in the sixties," I took up for myself.

"Yeah, like what?" they all asked in unison.

In my best sixties' voice, I laid it all on the line, "Well, I remember cutting a rug at the sock hop and having a blast doing it. We could really get down doing the twist and the limbo. Man, we really got our groove on. Then we would slip into our skates and rock and roll around the rink till someone yelled, 'Everybody skate backwards,' and we would, until it was Hokey Pokey time. Gee whiz, we really had a gas."

Giggles exploded as I stopped for a second. My grandkids were looking at me as if I had lost what little mind they thought I had left. I continued, not missing a beat.

"Back in the good old days, I would get all decked out with my best white go-go boots and A-line mini-skirt. Sammy said I looked real foxy. I told him he looked like a hunk himself in his flat-top and cool duds."

"Yuck!" Kylie exclaimed, and Austin high-fived her and added a fist bump for emphasis, but I was on a roll and kept right on rolling.

"We would get into Sammy's cool ride where I called dibs on the middle. I had to sit aside the gear shift, but it was worth it to sit by Sammy. I would grab the gear knob and shift the four-on-the floor on that '63 Chevy. My best friend called, 'Shotgun!' so everyone else crammed into the back seat. Sammy popped the clutch, and we laughed when he gassed the foot-feed and burned rubber. He really laid a patch behind. He was smoking hot as he peeled off and let those glass-packs rip. We all met at the Triangle to hang out and tell lies till the fuzz would tell us to break it up. Then we would mosey on down the road to the rock pile. On the way, we would play chicken up and down the strip with his best friend's car full of Cool Cats. Of course, Sammy would always win because he had guts made of steel. When it got dark, we would cruise Wesley and drag Lee where we would blow the doors off everyone else. If we came to a halt, we would jump out of the ride and do a Chinese Fire Drill, or see how many people we could stuff into a phone booth.

"Meanwhile, back at the ranch, my old man was going ape. He was fit to be tied when I walked in an hour past curfew. When my daddy-o yelled, 'You are cruisin' for a bruisin',' I wanted to say, 'Don't have a cow,' but I knew to keep my trap shut. Well. . .almost. . . I would have had it made in the shade—if you can dig what I am laying down to you—but I couldn't help but spout off to the pops, 'I didn't mean to rattle your cage. I was just hanging out with the gang.'

"But he was so uncool about the whole thing, so I got the royal shaft and was stuck in Nowheresville for a week—grounded to the pad—without my Princess Fone or Transistor Radio."

I stopped to take a breath, and my three grandchildren were staring at me in disbelief. I expected them to call the men in the white coats any second. They are coming to take me away, aha, aha!

"Sorry, guess I got a little carried away. Anyhow, I digress. But when you think about it, it doesn't matter what generation you speak, parents can be such party-poopers when you just want to get your chill on."

"U-m-m, you said, poop!" little Kylie squealed as she and Katelyn fell on the couch in hysterics.

I expected Austin to grab the girls, run to his room, and lock them in it until his parents returned, afraid to be within ten feet of his lunatic grandmother. But instead, he laughed heartily and said, "I think you are awesome, MiMi!"

"Awesome?" I smiled. Now that is a word I could understand in any lingo!

Part Four

The Good Old Days?

Ecclesiastes 12:1
Remember your Creator in the days of your youth.

33

Farm Living Was The Life For Me

VICKI

Farm living was the life for me—not that I knew anything else. Being born and reared on a dairy farm in South Sulphur, Texas, I can relate to the saying, "It was the best of times; it was the worst of times."

Grandpa and Grandmama took care of my older brother and me, while my mother worked to make what she thought would be a better life for us—but I loved life just as it was.

In the house lived my aunt, six years older than me and my uncle, four years older than me. Funny thing was my grandmama and my mama spent the next six years alternating who would have the next child, which I have heard wasn't a very unusual scenario back in the olden days.

But in today's times, having a baby boy (my brother), the next year your mother having a baby boy (my uncle), then you having the cutest little baby girl in the world (*me*), then your mother once again giving birth (my uncle) a year later, is almost unheard of, or at least in these here parts.

I soon learned to rough house with the best of them—for survival! To the guys, I was just one of the boys. But one day, Grandpa threatened my brother and uncles, "If you hurt that girl, you will see the rough side of a razor strap!"

Not knowing I had learned to fight back as well (or better) than the boys, Grandpa kept an eye out for any signs of distress. But after one particular incident where I took one uncle to the ground with a block to the back of the knees, he threw up his hands and let us fight it out. Because they loved me, they never hurt me too badly—or maybe it was the fear of the leather strap that kept me safe.

During the good old days, I learned the true art of *Indian rope burns* (grasping the victim's wrists in both hands and twisting the hands in opposite directions), *Noogies* (taking the knuckles of the fore and middle fingers and rubbing hard against the surface of the scalp, pulling skin and hair as you dug in harder), *Uncle*, (bending the arm behind the back till I hollered, *Uncle*), and not to mention, *Towel Snaps* and *Wet Willies*. I have to admit I got really good at all of them—striking before struck.

When we weren't fighting, we had great fun playing together outside. We learned at an early age that sticking our head inside the screen door led to "Come on in here and help me with the chores. I've got a list a mile long," so we busied ourselves with games like kick-the-can, hide-and-go-seek, or jumping out of the hayloft into the haystack (or in my case, being pushed out of the hayloft into the haystack.)

Food was hard to come by in the late 1950s. Snacks consisted of day-old-bread and mayonnaise sandwiches. Of course, that meant we had to go into the kitchen with the threat of chores waiting. So mostly we would run off to the pear orchard or pecan grove and fill up on green pears or pecans. The world was our smorgasbord.

Soon, the growls of our over-stuffed stomachs filled with too much green fruit lead to the realization we had overreached our quota. Then, it was a race to the outhouse, all of us in dire need of more than a one-holer!

"Hurry up!" was followed by a barrage of fists pounding on the privy door. We went through many a Sears-Roebuck catalog or corn cob wipes before we learned to curb our appetites.

Then just when we thought we could throw up (or worse) no more, we took a ride inside an old tractor tire and proved ourselves wrong. As we squealed with glee, we didn't realize how dizzy we were until we stood and staggered to the cold, green grass on the side of the hard, black pavement.

Then, it was on to line up to the electric fence, joining hands, finding a volunteer to grab hold and see how far down the row we could shock ourselves.

Finally, we heard the cow bells and knew we could avoid our chores no longer.

My favorite Holstein, Buttermilk, was mooing loudly to be relieved. So walking carefully to avoid cow patties (did I mention we spent our lives barefoot?) I sat on my little stool. I grabbed a teat in each hand, balanced the bucket between my legs, and swished the milk into the bucket. With a squirt or two to the mouth and a couple into the eyes of my siblings, I filled my bucket for my grandpa to pour into the milk cans. No electric milking machines were heard of in our dairy. Grandpa, however, did allow one piece of modern technology into the barn. He played soft music on an old Philco radio because he had read, "Good milk came from contented cows."

All that milking in the hot, dusty barn worked up a thirst. We would race to drink out of the rain barrel, and having learned the fine art of how to hold the ladle without getting a single wiggle worm in our mouths, we drank to our heart's content, which usually led to a race back to the outdoor toilet.

And oh, the Easter egg hunts that we had down in the pasture. The adults hid the hard-boiled colored eggs, and the excitement as they took their time almost killed us. All our cousins would join us for the holidays, so twenty or more kids ran, grabbed (and yes, more times than not) wrestled for the prize eggs, which usually had a quarter taped to them. I always could spot an egg with money. I would sneak up and grab the eggs out of my brother's basket, curl up in a little ball, and hold on to those prize eggs for dear life, with the others pawing at my hands to get the coveted coins. Of course, everyone would make the older kids let the younger ones have them. Oh, they wanted to let us have it, all right!

Some people may have driven past that old dairy farm, and, seeing all those kids running around barefoot and half clothed from daylight until dark, shook their heads. They may have actually felt sorry for the poor people who lived there. We may not have had any ready cash, but there was so much love in that house, we felt rich beyond compare.

At night when we relieved ourselves in the white, porcelain pot, knelt beside the bed and thanked the good Lord for another day together, then snuggled under mounds of blankets, all was right with our world and for that, I am much obliged.

Yes, farm living was the place to be. . .until I was old enough for farming to get real.

34

A Helping Hand

SAMMY

I guess I was about eight years old, give or take a little, when I began my professional cotton-hoeing career. By professional, I mean it was the first time I was compensated for performing the task. Even then, I wasn't paid the full rate of fifty cents an hour.

You see, my production of weed reduction in the cotton was limited, so I was only paid twenty-five cents per hour for my efforts. My mama would have to work alongside me and hoe a row and carry my row. In other words, she would hoe her row, and then turn to mine to help me catch up. Sometimes, my older sister would be hoeing on the other side of me and would help, too. It was ten hours a day of hot, hard work.

As I got a little older, I could make a hand on my own. Being able to do so afforded me the opportunity to expand my career. Now, not only could I hoe cotton, I could pick it, too. I got to haul hay and pull corn. Sometimes I even drove a B-Farmall tractor from one field to another which allowed me to hone my tractor driving skills enough to shred pastures.

I hated every minute of it.

My extreme distaste for being down on the farm started skewing my thinking. I began having ill feelings towards the folks I did jobs for. They were the reason for me having to do the hard work associated with farming. Why didn't they just leave us alone? Every time one of them drove up to the house, I knew my back would be hurting by sundown.

To tell you the truth, though, I think seeing the way my mama had to work bothered me more than anything. That woman did any and every kind of job she could to provide for us. She worked in the fields, in nursing homes, and cleaned houses to name a few. I saw her come home bone-tired more than once from a day in the sewing factory. I thought maybe too much was expected of her, and that led me to put some of the blame for her lot in life on those she worked for.

Now, let me say, most folks we worked for were good folks. But haven't we all felt mistreated at some point in our lives by the ones who had the power? Or felt helpless because of the situation we were in? Maybe we harbored resentment for the pain and suffering our parents or grandparents had to endure. I know I did. I see things differently now, though.

It was as if one day the proverbial light bulb came on inside my head. All of a sudden it dawned on me, I shouldn't feel anger toward anyone for allowing me to work for them—I should be thanking them. If it hadn't been for them, I don't know how my family would have made it. I also realize some of the odd jobs they had for me, they could have easily done themselves, but they let me do them just to help me.

My mother would scold me if she knew I was lamenting about her working as she did. She would be the first to acknowledge being grateful to the folks who let her work for them and helped her along the way. I now embrace the hard knocks, trials, and tribulations that were a part of my family's life ever since my grandparents migrated to Texas from Kentucky. I believe their sacrifices made us better, stronger people.

There's no doubt people of every ilk have had struggles and suffered injustices. I grant you, some more than others. It is downright shameful the pain inflicted, both physically and psychologically, on folks down through the years. I also agree with the philosopher who said, "Those who cannot remember the past are condemned to repeat it." So we have to be careful.

But consider this. The past is the past. It can't be changed, no matter how we feel about it. All any of us can do is hope for, and work for, a better future. And to realize those hopes and dreams, there is something we all need to learn: No one can get to tomorrow if they insist on living in yesterday.

35

Chicken On The Bone

VICKI

*L*ooking inside my refrigerator, I was taken aback by the vast amount of food we had crammed on the shelves. I shook my head when I saw I didn't have enough room to place the fried chicken I bought inside. When I offered my three-year-old granddaughter a piece, she put her hands on her hips, turned up her nose, and refused to take a bite.

So I did what any good grandmother would do. I began to tell this little brown-haired, brown-eyed, spoiled cutie stories about what it was like *when I was young*.

"When we were growing up, Kylie, we didn't have much choice in what we ate. I never remembered thinking about it twice when my grandmama hollered, 'Time for supper!' We had to *take it or leave it*. I was so hungry it didn't matter what was on the table, I was digging in."

I waited a second for that to sink in, again handing her a chicken leg.

I was preparing my lecture about the starving children in Africa when I heard, "No, MiMi!" She shook her head in great disgust, looked at me like I was some primeval alien and continued, "Don't you know, we don't do chicken on the bone anymore!" She stood there with her lower lip pouted out, as sincere as she could be, and I had to stifle a giggle.

Now in her defense, she couldn't read yet. She could tell us what every sign said above all the restaurants we passed—and could quote the menus verbatim for each as we would drive up to the drive-through window—so maybe she was a product of her rearing.

As my mind went back to my childhood, I compared the difference. Recalling how little food there actually was on Grandpa and Grandmama's farm, I started to tell her about the time my grandmama wanted me to help her fix supper.

It was 1962, and I was as excited as I could be as I followed Grandmama out to the chicken coop.

It wasn't long before I couldn't believe what my eyes were seeing. Grandmama picked that chicken up by the neck and twirled it around two times and pointed for me to pick up the hatchet. I walked over and picked up the handle, horrified that I had just discovered the real reason behind the saying, "Walking around like a chicken with its head cut off!"

Almost as fast as I had picked up that sharp blade, I threw it back down and took off running, disappearing in an instant behind the butane tank. After yelling my name a couple of times, Grandmama laid the chicken's head down on the old tree stump, and hollered at my uncle to go find me and bring me back, because as much as she wished it weren't so, I lived there and must help with the ways and chores of the farm.

My uncle didn't have much trouble finding me because they had stood and watched me run behind that old rusted butane tank two minutes before. He put his arms around me and told me this was what we must do in order to put supper on the table, and it wouldn't take a minute, and then I could get back to playing while they did the rest.

Now I had cut many a kindling limb on that tree stump. Shaking I walked back, picked up the ax and told myself it was just another piece of wood for the fire. I took a deep breath, aimed that cold steel, closed my eyes, and swung it as hard as I could—praying Grandmama's fingers weren't still wrapped around that chicken's neck, and that I would get it right the first time. Luckily, when I opened my eyes again, Grandmama was there to hug my neck, kiss the top of my head, and swat me tenderly to go back to my playing.

She turned toward the house to do God only knew what to that chicken, and I picked up my corncob doll she had made me for Christmas a year ago and played like she was a Hollywood movie star—anything but a farmer's wife!

In the glisten of the blade, I was initiated into the realities of survival, and I swore I would never eat chicken again!

And I didn't—for about two hours!

I looked over at my uncle across the supper table when Grandmama brought out that platter of crispy fried chicken, oil dripping onto the dish rag we used for a hot plate, and the smell of heaven couldn't have been any sweeter than the aroma of that chicken.

Now, we hadn't eaten in about six hours, and my stomach was in starvation mode, so I completely blocked out that chicken incident as I grabbed for the first piece off that platter. After all, I was the baby girl of the family. I heard my uncle chuckle as he grabbed one, too. We were eating like kings, and oh, did it taste good!

Yes, I started to tell Kylie all this. But as I looked at her innocent little face when she begged, "MiMi, there just isn't anything to eat in here, so can we run to Kwik Chek and get us something real?"

I just laughed out loud, hugged her, grabbed my purse and headed out the door with her clapping with glee. For some strange reason, chicken on the bone didn't appeal to me that much right now, either.

36

Where's Maybell?

SAMMY

When I was growing up in the country, almost every youngster was a member of a 4-H club. I belonged to the Hogeye 4-H, which was named for the community where it was located. I was ten or so when my dad learned the 4-H clubs in the area were having a pig giveaway contest. All a member had to do was write an essay to the county extension agency explaining why they should win a pig.

Daddy encouraged me to enter the contest. His encouragement went kind of like this, "Get some paper and a pencil and write something to win a pig."

"But Daddy, I don't wanna. . . ."

"Write!"

So I wrote. I didn't care one thing about winning, but I wrote. I didn't want to take care of any animal, especially a pig, but I wrote. And wouldn't you know it? I won one of the dang things.

My Uncle Tom took me to the location in Greenville, Texas to get the pig. He helped me pick one out, and we loaded it in his truck and headed back to our farm in Hogeye.

When we got home, I took the little Duroc pig and put her in a pen. She seemed scared, so I got in the pen with her and patted her back and rubbed her belly. Soon she was calm and nudging up against me. It was right then I made a big mistake for a farm boy. I let an animal, other than a dog or cat, become a pet.

I named her Maybell, and I fed and petted her every day. And she grew. Sometimes I would let her out of the pen, and she would actually follow me around like a dog. I'd give her something to eat. She grew some more. I would sit down, and she would nestle up against me wanting to be rubbed and fed. She got bigger. Soon she wasn't my cute little pet pig. Now, she was my great big pet hog. She was about as big as she was going to get, and I was soon to experience what life on the farm was all about.

I got off the school bus one cold winter day and made my way to the pig pen to check on Maybell. I found the pen empty. Thinking she had gotten out and wandered off somewhere, I began looking for her.

"Maybell! Maybell!" I shouted, but she didn't come. I looked everywhere, but she was nowhere to be found. I ran to the house and saw Mama in the kitchen.

"Mama! Mama! Have you seen Maybell? Where's Maybell?" I asked anxiously.

Mama hesitated for a moment before answering, "She is over at your granddad's."

"Why? Did she get out and go over there?" I wanted to know.

"No," Mama stated in a measured tone. "They came over here and got her. Your dad and granddad took her for meat today."

"Took her for meat? What does that mean?" I demanded.

"You know, took her for meat. I don't know how else to say it—they butchered her."

A feeling came over me as I had never experienced.

"Butchered her? You. . .you mean they killed Maybell?" I cried, "How could they do that? She was my pet. I'll never forgive them!"

"Okay. That's enough! That is just the way it is. It is wintertime, and we need food to eat," Mama answered, letting me know the conversation was over.

I hated them! Daddy and Granddaddy for killing Maybell, and Mama for telling me. I hated Hogeye, the 4-H, the county extension agency, Uncle Tom for taking me to get Maybell, and though they had nothing at all to do with it, the Carl's Tasty Sausage meat-packing plant over in Whitewright. I hated them all!

I moped around and pouted for weeks. As is often the case, my hatred for the perpetrators of Maybell's murder lessened as time passed.

Besides, we had a new baby calf for me to look after. It was fun to feed and pet it, but Maybell was always in the back of my mind. I never named that calf, and although it would come up to me whenever I went into the pasture, I never allowed myself to get as attached to it as I had Maybell. I knew someday it would be gone, either sold or worse. I had learned the lesson of life. . .and yes. . .death on the farm.

Maybell had taught me both.

37

A Cardinal Sin

SAMMY

I've always liked birds. Their freedom of flight, beautiful songs, and colorful plumage appeal to me, and I'm lucky to have plenty of birds out where I live. We have blackbirds, sparrows, scissortails, mockingbirds, doves, quail, hawks, owls, buzzards, an occasional blue jay and lots of cardinals, or redbirds, as we called them when I was young.

It is the redbird that is my favorite, but I hardly ever see one that I don't recall what I did when I was about ten or eleven years old.

I was down by the trestle in a thicket of trees. I had my trusty B-B gun with me, and I am sure I was pretending to be Audie Murphy fighting off the enemy, or I may have been Gene Autry or Roy Rogers.

No matter. Whoever I was, I know I was saving America or winning the west with my sharpshooter skills.

As I crept stealthily through the woods looking for more bad guys, a redbird caught my eye. It was fairly high up in a tree, and I stopped to watch it. As I stood there, it would fly from limb to limb, but never fly away. Continuing to watch it, I was struck by its beauty, the red of its feathers especially standing out against the backdrop of trees. The bird continued to flit about, moving from limb to limb. Getting lower and lower, it finally lit on a twig about twenty feet from me.

I couldn't believe my eyes! It just perched there looking at me. Watching it closely, I began to pump my B-B gun to build up the air pressure. When I had pumped it as much as I could, I raised the gun, aimed at the bird and pulled the trigger. Pop! The cardinal fell to the ground.

I got it! I got it! I thought excitedly as I ran to get my prey. My elation waned, however, when I got to the redbird.

The thrill I had experienced seconds ago was gone as I stood there looking down at the now-still bird. A sense of remorse came over me as I stooped to pick it up. I held the still-warm body in my hands and immediately wished I had missed the shot. I wanted so much to take back that moment I had pulled the trigger. But it didn't matter how much I regretted it, I couldn't change what I had done.

I found a stick, dug a grave the best I could, and laid the scarlet body of the bird in it. I quickly covered it with dirt and leaves and hurried out of the woods, feeling about as shallow as the grave I had just dug.

I didn't know then why it bothered me so much, but I think maybe I do now. I think it was because the redbird wasn't doing one thing to provoke my shooting it. It was in its natural habitat, posed no threat to me, and probably didn't fly away because it wanted to divert my attention away from a nearby nest. Its only fault was that its beauty caught my eye.

The truth is, the excitement of the moment caused me to act, never thinking of how I would feel when the rush wore off.

Isn't that the way we approach life sometimes? Don't we sometimes jump head first into things without thinking them through? Haven't we all been in situations where we would have been better off to just walk away—and later regretted we didn't?

You know what? There might just be a life-lesson in my little story worth teaching my grandchildren. So listen up, kids. It is okay to have big hopes, dreams and aspirations. Go after life with all the gusto you can to achieve things you never thought possible.

I ask you to remember this, though. Some things aren't what they seem. Be careful what you are aiming for. And please, before you pull the trigger, think of the redbird.

38

The Word According To Mama And Daddy

VICKI

My parents and grandparents had to have a wonderful sense of humor to raise me. I imagine I have even tested the patience of God many times. We won't go into how I have tested Sammy's patience—might give him fodder for another chapter.

My parents/grandparents did their best to teach me right from wrong. Although they didn't quote biblical scriptures exactly as written, I realize now they got the message across, just with different words.

The Bible teaches, "Thou shalt not take the name of the Lord thy God in vain."

Or as Grandpa taught me, "You say bad words, and I will wash your mouth out with soap!" How was I to know *that* included the words, "Gosh Darnit?"

The Bible teaches, "Let there be light and there was light. And God saw the light, that it was good, and God divided the light from the darkness."

Or as Daddy taught me, "Turn off the light. Do you think we own the electric company? This is *ON*. This is *OFF*."

Sammy is still trying to teach me how to divide the light from the darkness.

The Bible says, "And Jesus went throughout every city and village preaching, and the twelve disciples went with him."

I am sure my parents would have taught it this way, "Jesus and the twelve disciples had to walk ten miles through the snow, barefoot, uphill, both ways."

The Bible says, "Prepare and make yourself ready."

My mother instructed it like this, "Be sure to wear clean underwear. You never know when. . . ."

The Bible teaches, "Be not conformed to this world."

Or, as my daddy taught me, "If all your friends jumped off a cliff, would you jump off one, too?"

In the Bible, the Israelites complained they had no food, and God sent them manna from heaven, and they still complained.

Well, my parents knew how to put an end to that really quick, "There are two things for dinner—*take it* or *leave it*. Just remember there are children starving in Ethiopia who would love to have chicken livers for dinner."

And my daughter is teaching her children the same thing, just in a more modern Mommyism, "You get what you get, and you don't throw a fit."

But all the things my parents said weren't to discipline. Where the Bible says, "I can do all things through Christ which strengthens me," my parents told me, "There is nothing you can't do if you want it bad enough and do it for good. We love you. We believe in you."

I was blessed for being reared by grandparents/parents who cared enough to correct me, loved me enough to tell me, and laughed *with* me—not *at* me.

My God, parents, husband, children, grandchildren, and all the rest of my relatives and friends I have encountered over the years made me who I am today—the woman that when she goes out into the world, she causes the devil to quake, "Duck, demons, she's loose—locked and loaded!"

39

Some Coal Oil, Sugar And Two Cow Chips, Please

SAMMY

I know if you watch any TV or read any magazines at all, you have noticed the number of advertisements for medicines. A prescription or an over-the-counter drug is available for anything that ails you. It is certainly a good thing to have all these meds at your disposal. This hasn't always been the case.

When I was a boy, if folks got sick or injured, usually home remedies were applied to the situation. Due to the lack of funds and the distance to the nearest medical facilities, doctors were used as a last resort for treatment.

For example, I can remember staying at my grandmother's house. One thing you learned when around Grandmother was *not* to cough or sniffle. If she thought you even had a hint of a cold, she would have you slathered with Vicks Salve so quickly, it would make your head swim—literally.

First, she would rub your back and chest with a generous supply of Vicks. Next, a big dab would be applied right under each nostril. Then, just for good measure, she would jam a healthy portion down your throat. The gagging and coughing experienced from that little episode caused deep-breathing and allowed all the medicinal qualities of the Vicks to reach the very deepest parts of your lungs, clearing them of any congestion.

I don't know if the Vicks really cured you, or if staggering around in a menthol-induced high just made you feel better. I suspect, though, the thought of receiving another treatment gave you the willpower to stifle any lingering sniffle or cough.

But that doesn't compare to another method of curing congestion I heard about years ago. I really didn't believe it, so I just dismissed it and never thought about it again until now. The method? Well, it was boiling cow dung to make cow-chip tea. Yes, I said it was taking cow patties or cow chips and boiling them in water, straining it several times and serving it as a warm drink to relieve chest congestion. Turns out, it's true. Seems the recipient of the tea would cough so hard that finally all the congestion would disappear or greatly diminish. Now I can believe that—I think I would cough up a lot more than just what caused the congestion if I was ever served that concoction.

Something else used quite often for whatever ailed you was coal oil—kerosene. It was used as a topical treatment to fight infections, treat cuts and rashes and applied liberally to relieve the itching of insect bites. It was also mixed with sugar and used for sore throats or coughs. The coal oil was the actual medicine. The sugar was used to soften the taste of the coal oil in the hope the patient wouldn't puke his guts up while trying to swallow it. Oh yeah, and just to put everything in perspective, it was also used as a fuel for lamps and stoves.

There were all kinds of treatments. I've heard my older brothers speak of Black Draught. I don't remember ever taking this one, but from their description, it was brutal. I looked it up, and near as I could tell, Black Draught was used primarily as a laxative. That didn't necessarily mean you actually needed a laxative, because back in the day, it was fairly common to get a good cleaning out as a cure-all.

Of course, we all remember Castor Oil, which tasted so bad it was used as much as a threat for discipline as it was for an illness.

The list goes on—baking soda mixed with water was good for an upset stomach—gargling warm saltwater helped soothe a sore throat.

If you happened to fall and received a bump or bruise, the most common therapy was to be told to "Get up and shake it off. It'll quit hurting after a while."

Babies were bathed in Dreft laundry detergent to help cure diaper rash or other dermal problems such as infantigo.

Speaking of babies, it wasn't uncommon to give birth to one at home. There were eight children in my family, and only the youngest was born in a hospital. Family members or neighbor women would serve as midwives to assist in the birth of the baby. After all, the women needed to be home. Who was going to cook and clean if the woman of the house went off to some hospital to just lie around for a few days?

A case in point: I have always been told that the day I was born, my mama was so busy working in the cotton field that she couldn't even be there. I am not sure that is true, though.

Yes, it is a good thing we can stop by the local store or pharmacy to buy something for a cold or a headache. It's wonderful most of us have access to good medical care.

I tell you, though; I sense that the times they are a-changing. We might be well-advised to remember some of these home remedies. There could come a time when they are the only medical treatment we can get.

Aw, I'm sorry; I didn't mean to end this article on a downer. Here, have some of this hot tea—it will make you feel better.

40

The Gift I Almost Forgot

VICKI

I love Christmas. I always have. When we were growing up, Christmas was a lot different. We were tickled to get fruit and candy. Grandpa had a large peppermint stick, and we would stand in line to get a piece of it as he gently broke it off. It was a real treat. We might get a couple small gifts. For that, we were excited. You see, we didn't know any better.

Unlike when my son was growing up, and I handed him the coveted Sears Catalog and asked him to pick whatever he wanted. Of course, I meant a couple of things. However, when I went back and asked him what he had chosen, he picked up the book and said, "I want this page. . . and this page. . .and this page." And like any good mother, I would try my best to get everything my children asked for.

Like the year Stretch Armstrong figures were the number one toys for boys. The toy was a large rubber wrestler filled with some sort of gel. Every time he saw the commercial on Saturday morning cartoons, he would yell at the top of his lungs, "That is *all* I want for Christmas. If Santa doesn't get it for me, I will just die."

He would tell everyone that Santa was bringing him Stretch Armstrong. Now, we didn't have the internet or Super Targets back then. It wasn't a matter of getting online or picking up the phone. No, I searched Gibson's, TG&Y, Howard's, and Kress, but to no avail. I was so stressed that he would be disappointed that I wound up at my mother's house and cried like a baby.

She just laughed.

I couldn't believe she was laughing at my plight. When I asked her what was so funny, lo, and behold, what did she pick up? This year's cherished Sears Catalog with the Stretch Armstrong in it, ready to be ordered. And where did she work? Yep—at the catalog department at Sears—so it was a given that she could get him one.

I will admit that he loved that Stretch Armstrong for a couple of years. Wherever we went, Stretch went with us. That is, until the day he decided to open him up to see what the swishy stuff was inside. Needless to say, there was no putting the gooey back inside, and Stretch no longer stretched. In fact, he was flat as a fritter. All this mother's want-to couldn't put poor little Stretch back together again. And it was just his luck, Stretch Armstrong was no longer the have-to-have toy in the Sears catalog—he was so yesterday. My son had to learn the valuable lesson that there are just some things Mama can't fix.

Then, there was the year the Cabbage Patch Doll was the *it thing* that my daughter just had to have—or she *would die*. The marketing genius that Coleco was, they put out the little people after the catalogs had been printed. Commercials drove parents from store to store in desperation. Mothers were frantic to get the toys—and Lord knows my mother and I tried.

We would get up early only to find people had camped out overnight at any store that advertised they would have ten dolls the next day. We witnessed fist fights as mothers fought over the coveted prize. To our credit, we weren't that desperate.

My mother bought a pattern and made a doll as close to the Cabbage Patch image on the television as she could. To make up for it not being an original manufactured CPK, she made her two. I loved her dolls, but was concerned over the fact that Christmas morning would come, and the one gift Santa was supposed to bring my little girl wasn't going to be under the tree.

Finally, the dreaded day came, and my daughter opened her present. The look of disappointment broke my heart. She looked up at me and cried, "What does Santa think he is trying to pull? These aren't Cabbage Patch dolls!"

For once, I was speechless and buried my head in my hands, as the tears flowed freely down my cheeks. I had tried so hard. It was that day she would learn that there are just some things Mama can't fix.

As I cried, I felt a little hand on my shoulder. When I looked up, my little girl said, "I am just kidding, Mama. I know Santa (wink, wink) tried to find me a Cabbage Patch doll."

And with that, she picked up the twins, skipped into her room, and got ready for Sunday services. Of course, all the way to church, I was obsessing over the moment we would walk into the church, and there would be all the girls proudly holding their Cabbage Patch babies, and my daughter would have her homemade ones. But when we walked into the sanctuary, what did I see? A Sunday School room full of homemade dolls. Luckily for all of us, no one else had been able to find one, either.

As they compared all their babies, she beamed the brightest because Santa had brought her twins.

While we sat in church that morning, I took my son's little hand in my left hand and daughter's in my right, and thanked God for the real reason for the season. You see, I should have known better.

I had lost sight that the greatest gift we will ever receive will never be found under a Christmas tree. It is far too valuable to be stored in any other place, but in the depths of one's heart—the gift that Jesus had been born, lived and secured God's promise of our infinite tomorrows.

Yes, there are some things Mamas just can't fix. But— luckily for us—with that promise, we don't have to.

41

Father Knows Best

SAMMY

I read a comment the other day about how the *joy* of Christmas has become the *job* of Christmas. Well, now I say, "Ain't that the truth?"

I don't want to go all bah-humbug on you. I mean, come on now, haven't we let this thing get a little out of hand? This time of year we spend almost every spare minute searching for gifts. If we aren't driving somewhere to shop, we are surfing the net for something to buy. If we aren't surfing, we are thinking about what to buy who. It totally consumes us. It truly is a lot of work.

I think folks could learn a little from my dad. I'm beginning to think he had this gift-giving thing right all along. He didn't much care if he got anything. Hence, for the most part, he wasn't all that concerned about giving anything. He let everyone else work themselves into a tizzy while he just chilled.

There sure weren't any incidents such as my children witnessed as they were growing up. They recently told me about how they would stay awake until the wee hours of the morning to peek out the window as I got the stuff they were getting from the jolly one out of the trunk of the car. Oh, how they would giggle as they listened and learned new words from me as I ineptly tried to put their toys together.

I'm certain when I was growing up, my dad slept snugly in his bed on Christmas eve, never having to worry about constructing toys, or if they were the right ones.

Daddy changed a little, however, when the grandchildren came along. Why, I even remember the time he gave my son a gift he picked out just for him. Jeff beamed as his grandpa handed him a box containing his present. He eagerly ripped open the box exclaiming with glee as he viewed its contents. It was a turtle! A real live—uh, well—it was a real turtle all right. Somewhere during the wait for Christmas the turtle's expiration date had passed. It was a nice gesture on Daddy's part—but he had forgotten a minor detail—air holes in the box. Oh well, as they say, it's the thought that counts.

As Daddy grew older, he began participating a little more in the family Christmas festivities. All his offspring that could would come home on Christmas day. We would all gather around the tree to open the gifts Mama had spent all year getting us. While we were checking out our bounty, Daddy would slip out of the room, then reappear with a big ol' paper sack containing his gifts for each of his grandchildren. He gave each one, no matter their age, the same thing: a humongous foot-long peppermint stick and sometimes, if he had it, a dollar bill. I can remember him beaming as each one of them gave him a hug, clutching the peppermint as if it was the best gift ever. You see, it wasn't his presents that were important to them, but rather his presence that mattered the most.

Think about it. Wouldn't it be better if our focus on Christmas was just being with the ones we love? Maybe getting just a few things for each other, not worrying about what or how much someone else is getting? Let other folks hock the farm to buy gifts. We could be more like my old man. You know, just sit back and relax.

Who knows? We might even have time to think about the real meaning of Christmas.

42

Belt Lines, High Heels, And Hot Sauce

SAMMY

I guess it was in the fourth or fifth grade when I was first made aware of such a thing as an initiation. We were sitting in class when we heard laughing and yelling coming from outside the classroom. There was so much commotion, the teacher allowed us to go to the windows to see what was going on. I'll be honest, what I saw was something I just as soon they quit doing by the time I entered high school.

There, standing in the street, were two parallel lines of boys with belts in hand. And just to the left of them was one line of younger boys looking a little nervous.

"What's happening?" we asked the teacher.

"Oh, that is just part of high-school initiation. The freshmen boys are going to run through the belt line," she replied.

We could hear the pop of the belts as they found their mark on the freshmen as one by one they ran as fast as they could through the line. We watched as some swiveled from side to side or held their hands behind them trying to lessen the severity of the blows. There was a little giggling in the room, but I don't think it was from any of the boys. Our only thought was one day it would be our turn to go through the line. And didn't the teacher say the belt line was a part of high school initiation? What else could there be?

I found out a few years later, when as a freshman, an upper-classman handed me a piece of paper. "What's this?" I asked.

"It is a list of things for you to wear to school Wednesday," he answered. "Oh yeah," he continued, "don't forget to bring a shoe-shine rag and some brown and black polish." I looked at the list: Woman's wig, skirt and blouse or dress, lipstick, rouge, mascara, powder, nylon hose, high heel shoes and padded bra.

I showed up at school Wednesday and joined the other freshman boys who were also adorned in various female attire. What an attractive bunch of cross-dressers we were, but we had a little to learn about being a lady. One of our first lessons was how to walk in high heels. We stumbled and staggered our way to the first class, most of us walking on the side of our shoes to keep from falling. We fell into our desk seats and sat attentively as our female teacher pointed out that we might want to put our legs together when we were sitting— or, at the very least, put on some gym shorts.

In between classes we spent the day shining upperclassmen shoes. We endured being pushed and shoved as we teeter-tottered our way around the school, being harassed and made fun of and doing push-ups at the command of a senior. But at least at the end of the day, phase one of initiation would be over. Phase two would be the next night in the gym.

As we gathered in the gym, we wondered why the lower windows were covered. We soon understood as we were told to strip down to our underwear. We were then blindfolded for the duration of the initiation.

Next we were grabbed by the hand, and the upperclassmen ran us through the gym blindfolded, only to be let go of when we ran head-long into a blocking dummy used for football practice. The initiation elation continued. We were placed standing on a bench with our hand resting on the shoulder of someone on each side of the bench so we could maintain our balance. The bench would be lifted as high as possible by some guys on each end of it. When prompted, we were to jump off the bench. Not to worry, we would land on mats so there was no chance of being hurt.

I felt myself going higher and higher as the bench was lifted. The bench wobbled dangerously the higher it got. Soon, I could no longer touch the shoulders of the guys I was using for balance. I was blindly flailing my arms through the air as I struggled to keep from falling. Then came the command, "Jump! Jump!"

I took a blind leap of faith, only to quickly land face down on the gym floor. The sorry suckers had lifted the bench only about a foot off the floor, squatted down slowly until our hands no longer could reach them, giving the impression we were being raised much higher than we actually were.

The frivolity kept going as we drank from a bowl filled with lemonade and Baby Ruth candy bars. Close your eyes and try to visualize how appetizing that looked. We were given hot sauce to eat until our mouths burned, then offered water laced with alum to quell the burning in our throats. That concoction immediately caused our mouths and throats to go numb and constrict. The ingenuity of the upperclassmen was amazing as they kept coming up with things to do to us, most of which I can't tell here.

Finally, the initiation was over. We had done it! All in all, it hadn't been that bad, even kind of fun when you really thought about it.

And the dreaded belt line? Well, it had been discontinued only the year before. What a shame. It had always been such a big part of the initiation tradition. But maybe, just maybe, if we lobbied hard enough we could get it reinstated—for next year's freshmen.

43

Maria

SAMMY

*M*y classmate couldn't contain his excitement as he told me about the girls he had met over the weekend. In fact, this one girl, Maria, had even asked him to a party at her house on Saturday night. There would be several girls there, so if I wanted to go with him, I could. Of course, I wanted to go. There were, however, a few things that had to fall into place before the party could happen.

You see, Maria lived alone way out in the country with her dad who was a truck driver. Her dad didn't allow her to even be around boys, much less have a party for them. But on the night of the party, he was supposed to be on the road. All we had to do was make sure he was gone before we came to her house.

She didn't have a phone, but she did have a way to signal us if he wasn't there. We were to drive by her house, and if there were no lights on, that would mean her dad was gone. Also, she wanted one of us to call out her name so she would know it was us; then, she would let us in, and the party would begin.

It looked as if everything was a go as five of us pulled up to the darkened house. My buddy, who was driving, stopped the car several feet from the house, got out, and began calling Maria's name.

"Maria…Maria…*Maria!*" He called softly at first, getting louder each time.

Soon a silhouette appeared in the doorway. A voice answered, but it sure wasn't a girl's! It was a man yelling and screaming at us. Flashes of light became visible from the doorway, accompanied by the sound of POW—POW—POW! Screams of agony pierced the night as two of the guys fell to the ground and lay motionless.

Realizing the flashes and the sounds were gunfire, we took off like greased lightning. We ran right past the car and headed down the country road, running like world-class Olympic sprinters. When you are being shot at, self-preservation becomes foremost in your mind. Each of us strained to stay ahead of the others, knowing the one bringing up the rear would probably get shot first, thus, maybe giving the other two a better chance of escape.

Faster than a speeding bullet, able to leap barbed wire fences in a single bound, we soon found ourselves lying face down in a cotton field gasping for air. When I finally caught my breath, I spoke in a barely audible voice, "You know, I bet her dad found out about the party. I mean, a dark house out in the middle of nowhere with no other cars around, we should have known something was wrong. Why didn't we realize no party was happening?"

"I wasn't exactly thinking about logic. I was thinking about those girls," one of the guys said. "Hey, you know boys aren't able to think straight when it comes to girls," he declared.

"Do y'all think the other guys are dead?" I wondered out loud. "There wasn't anything we could do, was there? If we had stayed, we would have been shot, too. What good would that have done?" I rambled, trying to justify our running away.

"It's too late to worry about all that. We're in a mess. We have to walk to Leonard, find the police, and report this," the other guy rationalized. "And those other guys. . . ." his voice trailed off as we noticed car lights slowly coming down the road in our direction.

The car continued slowly toward us, coming to a stop almost straight across from where we lay. One of us whispered to the others, "Hey, that's our car! Maria's dad has stolen the car and is trying to find us!" We lay very still, hoping he wouldn't see us and drive away, but the car didn't move.

After a while the interior lights of the car came on as two people exited the vehicle. As they stood by the car, we could hear them talking and laughing—familiar voices—familiar laughter! It was our two buddies who had been shot back at the house! They got away! They were okay!

Excited and relieved, we stood up and called their names. When they saw us they began laughing so hard, they almost fell to the ground. It didn't take long for us to figure out what had happened. We had been had. There was no Maria. No girls. No party, either. It was all a joke, and it wasn't all that funny to us. You have to be pretty low-down to pull something like that on your friends.

The following Monday, I was sitting in study hall when the guy next to me whispered he had heard about the party some of us had gone to Saturday night at a girl named Maria's house.

Realizing he didn't know the details of what really happened, I seized the opportunity to tell him the party had been a real blast. "In fact, she's having another party this weekend, if you want to go with us," I told him.

"Sure, if the girls are pretty," he said. "And this Maria, what does she look like?"

"Oh, you'll be surprised at what Maria and the girls look like," I assured him. "I guarantee you'll be real surprised."

44

Big City, Let Me Be

SAMMY

When I was growing up out in the country, my travel opportunities were very limited. My trips consisted mostly of three destinations. One was six miles north to the annual Leonard Picnic, another to the State Fair of Texas in Dallas when the school took us on free admission day. Every now and then, we traveled to my maternal grandparent's house in DeQueen, Arkansas. That was about the extent of my journeys.

But as almost every young person from a small community knows, I wanted to see more and do more. I wanted to experience what was out there beyond the realm of my country comfort zone. I looked forward to getting away from Smalltown, USA—maybe go to a big city and have a little fun. I didn't know how I was going to do it, but I was going to make it happen. As it happened, the Army afforded me just that opportunity. After I finished basic training, I was assigned to a base near Indianapolis for more training. When I got off duty at the end of each day, a few buddies and I would go into Indy to get a little taste of big city night life. It was on one of those visits I learned city boys and country boys have some cultural differences.

You know, if you have ever watched a cowboy movie, and there was a fight involving a broken bottle, the proper etiquette for breaking said bottle is by banging it sharply upon a bar or a table.

Well, a guy in this place I was patronizing misunderstood my friendly, southern nature toward his female friend. Now, I was innocent as could be, but here's where cultural differences come into play—this guy evidently had never watched a cowboy movie.

I say this because he had a large bottle in his hand and broke it, not by striking it on some inanimate object that correct bottle-breaking procedures call for, but by hitting me right smack-dab in the face with it. As the bottle shattered, shards of glass stuck in various places on my face, and my lower lip was cut so deep, my friends took me to the base emergency room.

After getting my lip sewed back together, along with a stitch or two where some of the deeper embedded glass was removed from my face, I was released to go back to my barracks. Upon arrival, I went to the latrine to see just how bad I had been damaged. As I looked in the mirror, the reflection didn't reveal a pretty sight. I had several stitches and little cuts all over my swollen face. To this day, I sport a scar about an inch long on my lower lip to remind me of the big city fun I had in Indianapolis.

I guess that may have been the beginning of the end for my infatuation with big cities. Although I worked in Dallas for many years, I chose to commute the one-hundred-twenty mile round trip rather than move there. At the end of each workday, I always felt better as I viewed the Metro-Mess fading in the rear view mirror.

If I remember correctly, the theme song from the TV show *Green Acres* would also run through my mind, especially the part about farm living. He said it was the life for him. That's the way I felt. I just couldn't embrace city life.

Well, I guess the Good Lord was looking out for me in an unusual sort of way because the place where I worked shut down. It was as if God said, "Hey, you don't want to work in the big city? I can make that happen." The downside of all that was, I didn't know how I was going to make a living. The upside was no more daily trips to Dallas.

As it turned out, just at that time, my wife, Vicki, was offered the opportunity to buy the business she had worked in for many years. We decided to go for it, and I began working with her. *This is great*, I thought, *no more big cities for me*. That lasted about a week.

"We have to go to a company-sponsored event," Vicki informed me. "Oh yeah," she continued, "you need to start dressing a little better. You need to get a new suit to wear. The meeting is at an upscale hotel in *Dallas*."

"Did you say Dallas?" I asked. "Well, you can forget that, I'm *not* going to a fancy-dancy hotel in Dallas."

So a couple of evenings later, I donned my new JC Penney suit, and we headed for the hotel in Big D. Soon I found myself amid a bunch of people in suits, talking and laughing as they mingled with each other.

Being new to the coat and tie set, I stood off to myself observing how the men conducted themselves. I noticed almost all of them stood with one hand in their pocket, pulling one side of their coat back just so, exhibiting a professional, yet relaxed look.

Deciding I could emulate them, I walked over to join the crowd, hand in pocket, coat pulled back. I even propped my foot upon something to show just how cool and debonair I really was. It was working, too. I noticed how everyone was looking at me. It was only after I went to the restroom, I discovered why everyone was checking me out—my zipper had been open the whole time I had been there.

Since then, my country boy ways have embarrassed Vicki and myself in several cities. Once in San Antonio, a hotel employee and I had a foot race for about a block, he trying to carry my luggage, me refusing to let him. Vicki turned bright red, hands over her face, so no one could see who she was.

In Austin, I told a hotel clerk, "I guess we will just wear them," when asked what I wanted to do about our incidentals. I thought incidentals probably meant putting our jewelry in the hotel safe. How was I to know it meant how to pay for extra room service orders such as breakfast or snacks? I could go on and on, but you get the idea.

I've thought about how I could best explain how a big city makes me feel. I think I have come up with the best way to describe it. I think the last time I was in Dallas, I got a colonoscopy—that ought to do it.

45

And The Door Shall Be Opened

SAMMY

So there I was staring at a door trying to figure out if I could open it without having to pay. I couldn't slide under it, and if someone saw me trying to climb over it, I would look ridiculous. I had a gut feeling it would be in my best interest to spend some of my remaining finances on opening that door before I made a big mess of things.

I stuck my hand in my pocket to retrieve a dime, which was the cost of admission. I could feel the dime and the three quarters, which were the sum total of my wealth. I placed the ten-cent piece in the slot on the door and sighed in relief as it opened, and I entered the stall in the bus station restroom.

A dime? Come on, no one would go to such extremes to keep from spending a dime, especially if they were in my predicament. Normally that would be true, but when you are a nineteen-year-old soldier on a weekend pass who has spent all his money except for eighty-five cents, a dime means a lot. Here it was the middle of the month, and I was now down to seventy-five cents. It would be the first of next month before I received my eighty-seven dollars and fifty cents gross monthly salary. So yes, I needed that dime.

As I contemplated where I stood (or sat in this particular case) I was mad at myself for getting in this situation. I should have known better, but I was having so much fun that before I realized it, my money was gone. Also, I was painfully aware there was no one to bail me out of my dilemma. I sure couldn't call home—my folks didn't even have a phone. No need to write, either. The fact was my folks didn't have any extra money to send me. Besides, they ascribed to a *'You got yourself into it, now get yourself out of it'* philosophy of life.

I imagined this scenario would take place if I wrote home asking for a few bucks to see me through until I got paid:

*M*y little sister would find Mama lying on the floor gasping for air. "What's happening?" she would scream as she rushed to help her.

"Oh, I'm just exhausted from rolling on the floor laughing," my mother would explain while trying to catch her breath. "Here, read this letter from Sammy Tate."

My sister would read the part about my asking for ten dollars to help me through the remainder of the month. She would fall backwards into a chair, holding her side to keep her laughter from splitting it.

"That brother of mine," she would exclaim as she wiped tears from her eyes caused by uncontrolled hilarity, "he always was the comedian!"

*O*h well, I thought as I snapped back to reality, *I'll make it. The army gives me a place to stay and feeds me. Thank goodness, I had* *enough sense to buy a round-trip bus ticket so I can get back to my post. Yeah, I'll be all right.*

Just then I looked down to the right of the place I was occupying, and I couldn't believe my eyes—or my good luck! I'm serious, because there on the floor was a wad of money! I leaned to the right and grasped the dollar bills. I eagerly began to count my newfound fortune—one dollar. . .two dollars. . .three dollars. . .four! My gosh, by the time I quit counting, I had seven one-dollar bills in my hand! At that moment, I felt like a king on his *throne*!

I quickly stuffed the money in my pocket, afraid that in my excitement I might get it confused with the toilet paper. I left the restroom and checked when the next bus to Ft. Polk was leaving. I took a seat to wait and thought of all the events I had just experienced, when it occurred to me—the money wasn't mine. But there was no way I could find who it belonged to was there? Anyway, anyone who could afford to walk around with seven dollars rolled up in his pocket where it could drop out probably didn't need it, I rationalized.

After all, I was the one smart enough to invest in finding the money. Okay, I didn't have much of a choice, but it did cost me a dime. So by all rights, it was mine, wasn't it?

Still, I felt a little guilty, so I did what any good Texan would do—I walked over to the dining area and ordered a two-dollar chicken-fried steak and a big ol' glass of iced sweet-tea. I hadn't eaten since the night before, and it was now after lunch. I didn't know what manna from heaven tasted like, but that steak had to come close. As I filled up on the comfort food, I thought about the guy who lost the seven dollars. You know what? I bet he would be glad to know a soldier found it. Hey, it could be his way of thanking me for my service.

Well, I'll tell you, sir. You are mighty welcome, I thought as I washed down some steak with a big swig of tea, and *YOU will never know how much I thank you.*

46

Elvis, You Are A Friend Of Mine

SAMMY

I like music. Rock, gospel, blues, jazz, or country, it makes no difference to me as long as it is good. I have CDs by The Eagles, Dwight Yoakam, Nora Jones, Charlie Daniels, and ABBA to name a few. Of course, I like all of those, but there is only one singer I have almost every recording he ever made. I am talking about—yep, you guessed it—Elvis!

Not only do I have CDs, I have thirty-three and a third albums, forty-fives singles, cassette tapes and video discs of him. I even have *The Elvis Channel* on the radio in our car—all Elvis, all the time. I know, I know. I'm a little obsessed, but I have been listening to him for over fifty years (can that be right?) and I just never tire of his songs. To me, he is the best singer/entertainer there ever was or ever will be.

I first saw him on *The Ed Sullivan Show* when I was nine or ten-years-old. I had heard him on the radio, but to see him, well, that was something else! He had his dark hair combed back and with those long sideburns—I tell you, he was one cool cat! I sat there mesmerized as he sang his song, and the girls went wild. From that day forward, I was hooked.

I sang his songs everywhere I went. The woods and pastures, the cotton patches and corn fields were alive with the sound of his music. I serenaded the rabbits, squirrels, and coyotes with *Heartbreak Hotel* and *I'm All Shook Up*. Everything from rats to chickens was being exposed to the music of *The King*. I even gave a concert to the cows and pigs. Singing from the loft of the barn with an ear of corn as a microphone, the non-canine bovines and porcines seemed somewhat confused as I belted out *You Ain't Nothing but a Hound Dog*. Still, the cows looked at me all moo-moo eyed and the pigs squealed with delight when I swiveled my hip and curled my lip while running my fingers through my greased-back hair, being very careful not to touch and smear the long sideburns I had drawn on with Mama's eyebrow pencil.

As I got older, I continued being a fan. The more I learned about him, the more I liked him. In fact, I always thought if I could have met him and got to know him, we would have been buddies, maybe even best friends. I'll give you a minute to quit laughing. Through? Okay, here's why.

Elvis and I have a lot in common. For instance, he was raised in rather poor circumstances. One example I read was when he was a boy in Mississippi his folks moved from ramshackle house to ramshackle house before the rent was due because they couldn't pay it. Likewise, I was brought up in such squalor that once a thief broke into our house, took one look around and instead of stealing anything, left us ten dollars.

There are other similarities. He sang a song named *Little Sister*. I have a little sister.

He was tall and good-looking. . .I am tall and. . .well, I am tall.

Elvis' daughter's middle name is Marie. My mama's middle name is Marie.

One of his closest friends was nicknamed, Red. Red was my daddy's nickname.

At one time Elvis earned a living driving trucks. I used to make a living loading trucks.

He was in the Army and was stationed at Ft. Hood, Texas, for a while. I was in the Army and was also stationed at Ft. Hood. He was an E-5 in the 3rd Armored Division. I was an E-5 in the 1st Armored Division.

So you see, he and I are practically the same. I hope I don't sound egotistical when I point out that except for his fame, fortune, good looks and talent, it would be hard to tell us apart.

As I think about it, I could have easily been one of his running buddies in the Memphis Mafia or even been a part of his concerts. On one of his live albums, he introduced his band and his back-up singers. He even included the guy who handed him his towels, scarves and water during the show. *I could have been that guy!* I know how to hand out towels and carry water.

One of my regrets in life is that I never saw Elvis in person. Every time he was in concert in Dallas, I meant to go, but never did. My opportunity ended on August 16, 1977, when he was found dead at age forty-two at Graceland in Memphis. I will say this, though. Elvis may have left, but his music will live forever.

It's a shame we never got to meet, because he has been such a big part of my life. But who knows? Maybe someday we will. If that ever happens, I know exactly what I will say. I'll say, "Elvis, for all the songs we sang and all the good times we shared, thank you. *Thankyouverymuch.*"

Part Five

Life's All That. . . .

Ecclesiastes 3:1 For everything there is a season, and a time for
every matter under heaven:

3:4 a time to weep, and a time to laugh;
a time to mourn, and a time to dance.

47

Death Wishes

SAMMY

"*D*ad, wait until you hear this," my daughter warned me. "You'll just die!"

"Well, then I had rather not hear it," I replied. "I'm not ready to go just yet."

"Oh, you know what I mean. It is just an expression," she explained, rolling her eyes at my attempt at humor.

Of course, I knew it was just a way of telling me she had something really cool for me to hear. I use the same expression sometimes. At that moment, it occurred to me how we use rather serious words in very cavalier ways, especially words about death or violence.

I tell you what, let's review a few of the terms and phrases we use without even thinking about the serious consequences that would transpire if what we said really happened.

Let's begin with eating. How about this one? "Oh, his barbeque is to die for."

Yep, it is—eventually. Eat enough of the stuff and your arteries will be so clogged. . .well, you know. Seriously though, would you willingly die for some brisket? Isn't there something grander for which you would lay down your life? Something like, oh, I don't know, maybe chicken-fried steak smothered in gravy?

Here's another one: "I'd kill for a bowl of ice cream."

Really? I can see it now. You're loading up one of your home-defense AK-47s. Your wife asks you where you are going, and you reply, "By gosh, I'm going to go get me some ice cream and ain't nobody gonna stop me!" You might want to dial back on the aggression just a little. You would probably be better served to just buy a pint of ice cream without the violence, or you will be including Blue Bell for your last meal right before being executed.

Let's keep going. How about, "If I could win the lotto, it would tickle me to death!"

Okay, how would that happen? How does winning a large amount of lucre translate into being so happy it results in the demise of the ticket holder?

Maybe it would go something like this: You match the first number which causes a little grin. A smile emerges as the second number is also a match. The third one causes a giggle, and the fourth match has you laughing out loud. Now you're looking at the fifth match, and you are guffawing so hard your side is aching. Then when you realize you have matched all six numbers, it puts you in such a state of nirvana that you are gasping for air. In your state of delirious elation you need a drink of water to calm down. As you step toward the sink, you slip on the lotto ticket you unknowingly dropped. This causes you to fall headlong into the counter, hitting your head on the edge which, sad to say, kills you. But your statement has come true. You have won the lotto, and you also have just been tickled to death.

What about advertisements for movies or other events? The other night I wanted to watch a show on television, but decided to pass when told there would be heart-stopping action, and breathtaking suspense. Just call me chicken, but I didn't think either of those options was in my best interest.

Then there are sporting events: Football fans yelling to "Get out there and kill somebody!" Or "Take the quarterback's head off!" So help me understand. The desire to win is so great that you are encouraging people to actually kill for the victory. And because he can pass a ball, it wouldn't bother you to see a young man carted off the field minus everything above his shoulders.

Listen. I know *killing someone with kindness* is meant in an endearing way. And *it will scare you to death* is just a term to sell tickets to a haunted house. I also know my tongue-in-cheek look at all the phrases I have written about today aren't meant to be of any harm. In fact, probably aren't. Still, I can't help wondering if we were to substitute nicer, more caring words for those denoting death or violence, it could result in a kinder, gentler society.

Hey, it wouldn't *kill us* to give it a try.

48

It's Enough To Make The Indian Cry

VICKI

I am not a morning person, so when the church adopted two miles of highway to keep clean, my first thought was to say, "Have fun," and sleep in. But I am cursed with the inability to see a need and not fill it. Guess that isn't a bad thing to be cursed with, but at 7 a.m., it sure was tempting.

When the alarm went off, it was still dark outside. I pulled the cover over my head, but I had made Sammy promise to make me get up—and darn it, he is cursed with the inability to not keep a promise.

Soon we met up with the rest of the gang in front of the church. Gloves on, water packed, and sunglasses on the ready, we split into four crews, half down one side and half up the other. The goal was to meet in the middle. How hard could it be to pick up two miles of trash?

After all, I hadn't really noticed much debris in the ditches. Figuring we would pick up a kitchen sack full and be done in fifteen minutes, I almost swallowed my teeth when our supervisor handed us each a forty gallon, heavy-duty commercial grade trash bag. Still thinking she was being over-zealous, and praying she wasn't doing that from her past experiences (I had happily already scheduled something for the day of the last pickup) I smiled and took it—never imagining in my wildest dreams people would actually throw trash out their vehicle windows—on purpose. I figured we would just be picking up the stuff that blew out of the back of people's pickups.

We drove down to the starting point two miles out, and I had no sooner gotten out of the truck and crossed the road, when I almost stepped right onto a dirty diaper. I looked at the diaper and looked back at the youth—who were just getting out of their pickups, and did what any older, more mature person would do—I acted like I didn't see it and headed for the Styrofoam cup lying on the ground ahead of me. From behind me I heard a youthful voice, "Vicki, you missed this diaper."

I didn't even look back, just hollered, "It is your turn. You haven't even begun to pick up diapers, and I have slung way too many in my lifetime."

When I turned back to the task at hand, what lay ahead of me made my skin crawl. Is this what America had been reduced to? I could understand the weathered shingles which had blown off someone's house, the lost trailer license plates, and even the hubcaps which had been displaced by a bump in the road, but it was the fast-food cups, plates, forks, napkins, spoons, old ropes, box of wood scraps, beer cans and bottles, a million cigarette butts, and the mounds of Styrofoam that broke my heart.

Hoping against hope it had all been accidental, I looked up just in time to see a car pass by, a hand deliberately appear out of the window and throw a bottle our way. I had to remind myself I was representing the church, there were teenage kids all around me, and the car was way too far in front of me to hear the things I *wanted* to say, anyway.

As my blood pressure soared out of control, I was thankful for my husband who was in rare form and centered me back to a state of mind I could understand.

One of the boys went over to pet a horse, and Sammy said, "That horse will hardly talk to you in front of people."

The lad had never heard of Mr. Ed, the talking horse, of course, of course, so my husband's humor went right over the boy's head. I got a big chuckle out of it, though.

A short time later, I looked up to see the girls pumping their fists, soliciting a honk from a passing diesel. When the driver obliged and pulled on the horn, the boys and girls clapped and laughed.

Sammy hollered, "Boys, I don't know if you know it or not, but those truckers were *not* honking at you." Looking over at the pretty young ladies, the boys nodded their heads in agreement.

Chasing the girls with spiders, coke bottles used as spittoons, several more dirty diapers, and what we thought was a snake skin (turned out to be a waste disposing tube from an RV) the boys were having fun watching the girls run and squeal with glee.

Sammy said, "When you get home, pull up You Tube and listen to the song *I Don't Like Spiders and Snakes* by Jim Stafford. You will hear a girl warning a boy, 'That ain't what it takes to love me.'"

This time, they got the joke.

After a few hundred feet, back aching and sweat pouring, Sammy looked up to see buzzards overhead. He punched me, "See there, Honey, they are just waiting. They know the old people are helping today."

Yes, thankfully, I had the kids and my husband to take my mind off what all we had just picked up along God's beautiful grassland. If not, I am afraid I would have had a stroke just thinking that people could take this wonderful world for granted like that.

As we unloaded one sixty-gallon, heavy-duty, commercial trash sack after another (twenty-five in all) to place under the sign that read *Adopt a Highway Next Two Miles, Celeste United Methodist Church,*

I tottered between being so proud of my congregation, to being so angry that the apathy of others made the act necessary.

The Texas-born program is now in forty-nine states and saves the country almost a quarter of a billion dollars a year, with over eight million pounds of trash being picked up last year in Texas alone.

So please, for God's sake, the next time you start to throw something out the window, Don't Mess With Texas, Keep America Beautiful, and Don't Make the Indian Cry!

49

Angel In The Mist

SAMMY

It was already dark with a light mist falling when I stopped at the store. As I got out of my vehicle, I noticed a car with the hood up at the far end of the parking lot. I could see two people bent over doing something to the engine. I didn't think much about it as I went into the store to make my purchase.

When I exited the store they were still there. For just a moment I thought about offering my assistance, but decided against it. After all, I had worked late, and it was Friday night. I was tired and just wanted to go home. Besides, what could I do? I wasn't mechanically inclined, and someone else would probably be along if they needed help. I reached for the handle on my truck door just as one of the guys stood up and fell against the front of the car, frustrated.

"It's never going to work," he said, "It's stripped."

I tried to ignore them as I got into my truck. I sat there for just a moment fiddling with my keys, watching them as they discussed their situation. *Oh, what the heck*, I thought, *I can't leave without at least knowing if I can help.* Getting out of my truck, I walked over to the young men and asked, "What's the problem?"

"Well, the bolt that holds the alternator in place is stripped, and we can't tighten it. We've gone as far as we can go with the alternator belt slipping like it is," one of them answered. "You don't know where we could get a bolt like this, do you?" he asked, holding the bolt up for me to see.

"I sure don't, and there's nothing open here in Celeste," I answered. "The closest place you could get one would be about fifteen miles from here in Greenville. I don't know if any auto parts stores are open this late."

I could see the exasperation in their faces. "Do you know anyone around here you could call to help?" I asked. "If you do, you can use my cell phone."

"No man, we're from Longview," one answered, naming a town about three hours away. "We're just passing through."

"I tell you what. I'll get a phone book from the store and call around Greenville. If any parts store are still open, I'll take you to see if we can get a bolt," I offered. I borrowed the business directory from the store, turned to the yellow pages, and dialed the number of a parts store. We were in luck. It would be open for about thirty more minutes, giving us enough time to drive the fifteen miles before they closed.

I called Vicki to tell her what I was doing. "Are you sure? I mean. . .well, okay. . .but you better be careful," she warned.

One of the guys got in my truck with me while the other remained with the car. I'll be honest, I was a little apprehensive as we pulled away from the store. It was one thing to be with a stranger on a lighted parking lot, but quite another to be alone with him on a rainy, dark highway.

What am I thinking? This guy could be an escaped convict for all I know, I admonished myself. *Why didn't I just go on home?*

We drove along, neither of us saying anything. He could sense my nervousness. I would tense up each time he made the slightest movement. Finally, he broke the silence.

"Hey man, don't worry about me, I'm okay. I appreciate what you are doing for us." After he said that, I felt better, and we made small talk until we arrived at the store. He went in and came out smiling. "They had it," he said, obviously relieved.

"Are you hungry?" I asked as we backed out of the parking space and onto the street. "If you are, I'll buy you and your friend a hamburger. The store back in Celeste is closed by now."

"No, I better get back to the car. My friend is probably scared a little," he replied. That took me aback. I never considered someone being afraid in our small town. As I thought about it, he and his buddy were probably just as nervous about me as I had been of him.

We went along, again not talking, listening to the slapping of the wipers as they removed the drizzle from the windshield. After a while, his voice interrupted the sound of the wipers, "You know what? You're an angel, man. If you hadn't come along, I don't know what we would have done. In fact, Sunday morning when I go to church, I'm going to stand up and tell the whole congregation I met an angel on Friday night."

"I am far from being an angel," I said. "I'm just glad I could help."

By this time we were driving up to his car. I positioned my truck so its lights would shine on the engine, and I could jump-start the battery if the bolt did solve the mechanical problem. In a matter of minutes, they had the bolt in place and the alternator secure. He slid under the wheel and turned the ignition. The car fired right up without needing any assistance.

He stuck his hand out the window to shake mine. "Remember what I said in the truck?" he reminded me. "I meant every word. Tonight, you're our angel. Thanks again." With that, he backed up his car and pulled onto the highway.

I got in my truck and followed them down the road a short distance to make sure everything was okay. Seeing that it was, I turned around to drive home.

As I turned onto the road to my house, I reflected on what he had said to me, "Tonight, you're our angel." I kind of laughed at being called an angel. I had no wings. No halo, either. You know, for those guys, I might have been an angel.

That gave me a good feeling—a feeling that was. . .well, almost spiritual.

50

Youth Challenged

SAMMY

I don't know about this getting older thing. I've tried to ignore it, but it keeps coming at me. No matter where I go, or what I do there are reminders. Consider the following:

You are really reminded of your age when the bulk of your mail is AARP solicitations or from companies with the always uplifting sales pitch that asks, "Are you prepared for your final expenses? Send for a free brochure!"

Hey, make my day! Send me a bunch of them. I can't wait to read all about funerals and final resting places.

You know you're not a spring chicken anymore when you go into a clothing store to find something suitable to wear. You wade through aisles of clothing to find something you think might be appropriate for your age. Finally, you find it. It's one rack stuck over in a corner with about five shirts and a couple of pair of pants on it. The store clerk doesn't even offer to help you. She knows you're probably not going to buy anything. You're wearing a five-year old shirt, and your shoes went out of style about ten years ago.

It's even worse when you visit an antique store, and it's stocked with furniture, kitchen gadgets, tools and toys like you grew up with. I shopped in one recently that had an army uniform just like the one I wore hanging in it—*in an antique store!* It couldn't have been that long ago when I was in the service. . .let's see. . .I went in and uh. . . that would mean I have been out. . .oh my gosh! Can that be right? It's been that long?

"Uh, Ma'am. Is that chair to look at, or can it be sat in? I'm feeling a little tired."

As I sat down, Vicki walked by, looking for me. She didn't see me. I had blended right in with the other antiques.

A couple of years ago, Vicki and I participated in a walk to benefit the Arthritis Foundation. Some ran, some walked—we walked. We did it to support our niece who has arthritis. As we walked the three-mile course through the streets of Ft. Worth, I was quite flattered to have the young women stationed here and there to keep us on course come out and pat me on the back and tell me, "Good job," or "Hang in there." It was flattering until I looked around, and became aware I was one of the oldest people participating. It was then I realized the young women were so encouraging to me because they didn't want me falling out in front of them where *they* might have to do CPR on me.

You're probably on the downhill slide when you and a buddy are driving along and spot a pretty young woman on a riding lawn mower cutting grass. You elbow your friend and say, "Man look at that. Now, that is nice!" Your buddy smiles and gives an understanding nod. Sadly, he knows you are talking about the mower.

Or you are watching TV, and the announcer says all the details about the latest Hollywood sex scandal will be coming on next. You yawn and flip the channel to watch a show about lowering your cholesterol.

There are lots of ways that affirm you are getting along in years, but this is the best one I've heard. I was talking to a friend about the aches and pains you experience with age.

I told him that for no apparent reason I wake up hurting in a different spot almost every morning. He said, "I know what you mean. I guess you really are getting old when you wake up in the morning and realize you have injured yourself just by sleeping."

Another sure sign you are getting along in years is when you start telling the same stories over and over. As you begin relating another fantastic saga of your life, if you watch closely you can see the eyes of the recipients of your tale roll back into their heads, as they realize they are about to endure the same long-winded tale of when you were young.

Another sure sign you are getting along in years is when you start telling the same stories over and over. As you begin relating another fantastic saga of your life, if you watch closely. . . .

51

I'm One In A Million

VICKI

"*B-12*," I literally squeaked as I called out the game number during our latest Bingo Club get-together. "Sorry," I apologized, as I gulped down a large drink of my ever-present Route 44 Sonic cup of unsweet tea. *What was I thinking?* I wondered as it happened again on *I-30* and *O-69*.

I know I can't eat bread or cake in public as it gets stuck in my esophagus, causing me to shriek like a mouse when I talk. To take up for myself, I was busy having fun listening to the laughter and stories during the half-time break in our games, so I hadn't consciously eaten that large piece of sponge cake with strawberries and whipped cream that had been placed in front of me by an innocent helper.

"I am one in a million. . . ." I started to explain in that irritating voice which resembles fingernails on a chalkboard.

I heard murmurings of, "What in the world?" and "Do you need me to call numbers for a while?" coming from my fellow players. I paused, drinking an eight-ounce bottle of water in one gulp, washing down the cake which was sitting in my throat soaking up the liquid.

"No, I'll be all right," I comforted them, my voice returning to a semblance of normalcy. "You see, I have a disease. If I don't drink a lot, especially when eating bread or cake, my sphincter regurgitates my food back into my esophagus."

I admit my dark humor side took a little glee seeing the look of horror on the faces of my unsuspecting friends. Thoughts of my husband Sammy's column—on old people telling every aspect of their illnesses, and no one wanting to hear it—flashed clearly in my mind, but I was on a roll, and there was no stopping me now.

"I have this problem which I almost died from."

All eyes were fixed on me, and I definitely had their attention, even if it was leaning toward the horrified side.

"I had reflux a few years ago which got into my lungs, and it took six doctors to find the cause. I was very, very sick—*if they did not find a cure soon, just let me go to Jesus*—sick. Finally, a specialist made me swallow a camera which passed through my throat, stomach, and intestines . . . and what they found . . . ."

I paused for the full effect of my next explanation, ". . . . caused the doctors to rush me into surgery immediately—EndoCinch surgery—where the surgeon places an overtube over an esophageal dilator. He uses suction to capture a fold of tissue. While using the EndoCinch device (which resembles a miniature sewing machine), he stitches the tissue just below the lower esophageal sphincter."

"Say what?" they all yelled in unison. I saw the *You lost us at EndoCinch* look I have come to know and love and had secretly hoped for.

"I am just funning with you!" I laughed. "Not about the being one in a million. . .or the being sick. . .in laymen's terms, the top of my stomach that opens and closes to let food in and out is paralyzed, so I had to have surgery to fix it. I am *so* much better than I was. One of the downsides is I must drink six or more Route 44 Sonic cups of water/tea a day (about two gallons) or the food backs up into my throat, and I squeak like a mouse—as you have just heard. *Oh, yeah. . . ."*

I took a few drinks because the last two words sounded like a baby's squeak toy, ". . . .when it does that, it hurts! I was studied by several doctors because they couldn't find another case exactly like mine. My luck—I can't win the lotto—but I can get a condition that there is only a one in a few million chances I can get. Go figure."

Seriously, I get a lot of ribbing with the drinking. I have learned to laugh to keep from crying. Sammy says he is glad I can't drink alcohol, because he doesn't think he could afford me. The waitress at Red Lobster came by for my fifth refill in fifteen minutes and asked, "Does that glass have a hole in the bottom of it?"

I thought, *No, but your tip does*! But I just nodded and smiled.

To which Sammy told her, "To save yourself more trouble, why don't you just bring a water hose over here!"

My bingo partners' laughter only fed my desire to go on and on about the side effects of drinking so much, and what a barrel of laughs I am on vacation, having to stop every forty-five minutes to rid myself of 44-ounces of Sonic tea. . . and how my son-in-law's bladder is the size of a basketball, so when he travels with us, he can't see the humor in stopping that often at all. . .and how I have told Sammy that when I die, just save his money and bury me in a Sonic cup as it is my constant companion. . . .

But time-is-a-wasting, and there are games of Bingo to call and prizes to be won and stolen, so I leave that for another night.

As I called out, *I-29*, in my regular voice, I smiled to myself and silently wished I was twenty-nine again and didn't have to worry about sphincters, or surgeries, or Big Gulps. I continued calling numbers, stopping every so often to take a few drinks. Then it hit me—I hadn't made one pit stop in over an hour. As I excused myself, I sang, *This tea is not my home; it's only passing through. . . .* Literally.

52

Hiss Story

SAMMY

I was wiggling and squirming in my seat as the preacher talked about snakes in his sermon. He told of passages in the Bible that referenced them and personal stories of his encounters with them. Usually my being uncomfortable during the sermon is because the good pastor is stomping on my toes with the message he is preaching—but that wasn't the case today—it was the snakes. The very thought of them made me shudder. It bothered me so much, I stayed awake during the whole sermon.

Now let me say except for water, flying, bridges, high overpasses, caves, crowds, mountains, tall buildings and women, there isn't much that scares me. But snakes? Man, they give me the heebie-jeebies—all of them. I don't care if they are short or long, poisonous or non; they are all deadly, slithering menaces to me.

I am so freaked out by them, I can't even touch a rubber snake or look at a picture of a real one. If I see one on TV, I quickly close my eyes, losing any semblance of machismo as I meekly ask Vicki if the snake is gone before I can look again. And if a future dead snake shows up in my yard, I am so rife with fear, I can't get close enough to it to contribute to its demise by using a hoe. I have to get my shotgun so I can blow it to smithereens from a safe distance.

I don't like snakes.

I guess when it comes right down to it; it is the nature of snakes that causes me to have a phobia about them. They are such sneaky suckers. They can co-exist with you right where you are, and you will never even know it until you do something that upsets them. Then, they will strike quickly, causing pain and sometimes even death.

But as I think about it, I may be a little one-minded to pick on just the creepy-crawling snake that gets around on its belly, 'cause there are plenty of snakes that are upright and walking among us.

It's hard to distinguish them from the rest of the folks. Unlike the rattlesnake that shakes its tail to warn you of an impending strike, these folks don't have a rattler to let you know you had best keep your distance. But there are other signs that you are probably going to get bitten if you don't.

As with any snake, the flicking of the tongue is a good indicator something is about to happen. If you watch and listen, you will notice they hiss and moan at every turn, spewing their venom indiscriminately, not caring who or what their poison might hurt or affect. They are only happy when they are unhappy. And if they can make you or anyone else as miserable as they obviously are, then they are downright elated.

Here's the thing, though. If a snake keeps hissing—and striking—and biting—eventually the only thing it can associate with is another snake. Then you know what happens? Usually one snake will end up swallowing the other.

I don't like snakes.

53

Telecommunications

SAMMY

*M*y mother, Katie Marie, never learned to drive, which obviously limited her ability to get a lot of things done by herself. As she aged, she became even more dependent on family and friends to help her out in getting things accomplished. However, she wasn't completely without the means to make sure she got what she wanted and got them her way. You see, she had a powerful, powerful tool at her disposal—she had a phone!

She would call five, six, seven times a day. If she didn't get to talk to you, she would leave, not one, but several messages concerning the reason for her call. Each day when I got home and saw the light blinking on the answering machine, I could rest assured there would be a message from Mama.

Wondering what she wanted this time, I would take a deep breath and push the button. "Sammy Tate," she would say, "I ordered some socks for all you boys. I need you to come get a pair."

Pushing the button for the second message, I would hear again, "Sammy Tate, when are you coming by to pick up these socks?" The next message would be the same, as would the next.

Thinking I would just wait until the next day to go by for the socks, I would settle in to enjoy my evening. Just as I pulled off my shoes, the phone would ring, "Sammy Tate, do you want a pair of these socks or not?"

"Yes, Mama, I'll be over there in a minute," I'd answer, knowing I might as well go right then to get the socks. She wouldn't stop calling until I did, and it didn't matter to her what time or how often to call.

Like when I worked the night shift, I would get home about one in the morning, and not being one who could go straight to bed, I usually watched TV until I got sleepy. Around seven in the a.m., the phone would ring. It would be Mama. "Have you gone to pick up the mail?" she would ask, referring to me getting her mail for her when I went to the post office each day.

"Uh, no, Mama, I haven't. It's seven o'clock. I didn't go to bed until two, so it will be awhile before I go get the mail. Besides, the mail isn't even distributed until nine-thirty or ten."

"Well, when you go get yours, don't forget mine," she would remind me. An hour later there would be a repeat call asking the same thing. I didn't want to hurt her feelings, but I couldn't keep on functioning in a sleep-deprived state. So I took action to stop the early morning calls—I got my wife, Vicki, to call her.

"Katie, you have got to stop calling so early in the morning," Vicki told her. Mama defended her calls by stating she didn't call until *she* had already been up two or three hours.

"Yes," Vicki agreed, "but that is about the time Sammy is going to bed." Mama agreed to call later in the day, but reminded Vicki she needed her mail as soon as I got up.

Speaking of mail, I recall the time Mama called me because she hadn't received her social security check. "My check was supposed to come today, and I didn't get it!" she exclaimed in an upset tone. "I have been calling the post office all morning! No one answers! *I need my check!*"

"Mama, just calm down," I said, trying to soothe her. "Sometimes things happen to cause the mail to be a day late. You'll get it tomorrow," I assured her.

As if I hadn't even said anything, she continued, "You go to the post office to see if they have my check!"

"Mama, they don't have your check, so there's no need. . . ."

"*I want my check!*" she interrupted.

So I dutifully went to the post office and told the postal employee Mama's concern about her check. I explained she was quite elderly and was upset, especially since she had been calling the post office all morning, but got no answer.

"Yes, our phones aren't working for some reason," the clerk explained. "By the way, is your mother Katie Griffis?" he asked. "If she is, I know all about her check. She has already called next door to the Kwik Check and had someone come over here to find out about it. I think she's okay, now."

As I think back on it, it's funny now how I let her phone calls irritate me. Yes, they could be trivial, and she could be demanding; but really she wasn't asking much of me. I know it is easy for me to say because it will never happen again. But if I could push the button on that answering machine just once more and hear, "Sammy Tate, I need you to. . . ."

If I could. . .yeah, if I could.

54

A Couple of Suckers

SAMMY

I was backing out of a parking space at the doctor's office when a woman approached my car, motioning for me to lower the window. Thinking she might be having some kind of trouble, I complied. Before I could even speak, she began telling me about her husband having throat cancer. He was on the way to the hospital, and she just didn't know what she was going to do.

"Now, I don't want *no* money," she assured me. "I just want to get some food for my four kids. They've barely had anything to eat for days."

Well, as it happened, we were there because my granddaughter had a doctor's appointment. Vicki and I had dropped her and her mother off and went to get some takeout food for all of us. We had just picked the lunch up.

"Here," Stefani said to the woman as she offered her our unopened food order. "Take this for the kids. We'll get us some more."

This took the woman aback. She hadn't considered someone actually having food to offer.

"No, no," Vicki said as she reached into her purse.

"That's not enough. Take this money to get your family a good meal."

You could see the relief on the woman's face. That was exactly what she was hoping would happen. She quickly grabbed the money and took off down the street. We were going the same direction she was and watched as she waved the money at a man leaning against a post a half-block away. I assume he was her supposedly sick husband. I'm no doctor, but the guy didn't look all that ill. In other words, we had been had.

Sometimes I think Vicki and I have *Sucker* emblazoned on our foreheads. This stuff happens to us quite often. Like an incident that also happened in a parking lot awhile back. We were finishing loading our groceries in the car when a guy approached us asking for some money for enough gas to get home. He said his wife and kids were with him and pointed to a van a couple of rows over. He only lived a few miles away, and he was trying to get them home.

I was skeptic, but answered, "I guess so," and gave him a few dollars. He thanked me, and then turned to walk to the van. But that wasn't good enough for Vicki. She started chasing after him, more money in hand. When she caught up with him, I heard her tell him as he took the money, "We have been so blessed. We want to share our blessings with you. Please pay it forward when you can."

When we left the parking lot, we were three or four cars behind the van. As we followed it down the road, Vicki sighed contentedly; then said, "You know, it feels so good to help folks when they need it."

"It sure does," I answered, "but it would feel a whole lot better if he would have stopped at one of these gas stations we have been passing since we left the parking lot."

It doesn't have to be someone on the street or in a parking lot after your money. Most of us get solicitations either by mail or electronic media almost every day. We also are informed quite often of the misinformation, mismanagement, and outright theft at some of the charities. It can be hard to sort through which ones really deserve our contributions. No one likes to be taken advantage of, and when we are, it definitely affects our willingness to be generous.

Still, I would rather err on the side of compassion than not be willing to lend a helping hand at all. We all know people who couldn't care less about their fellow man. What they have they are going to keep. They wouldn't give a nickel to see a chicken pull a freight train, much less donate to a worthy cause or a needy person.

That's their right, but a word of caution. *Eventually, you reap what you sow. What you have today could be gone tomorrow. It could be you needing the helping hand.*

Where I used to work, we had a saying, *Doing the right thing wrong.* Meaning, of course, that even though you are well-intentioned, the way you do something may cause the end result to be worse than if you did nothing at all. That can even apply to giving.

Here's a case in point:

Vicki and I were dining in a restaurant. We watched a gentleman wearing a coat with large side pockets go from table to table putting leftover food in his pockets. He looked to be homeless. As I stuffed barbeque in my mouth with both hands, I began feeling a little guilty.

"Vicki, I think we should buy him something to eat."

She agreed. I went over to the guy and asked if I could buy him supper. He eagerly accepted. We walked over to the serving line where I told him to pick anything from the menu he wanted. It didn't take long for him to select the all-you-can-eat meal.

I walked over to the cashier, told him I was paying for an all-you-can-eat plate while pointing out the guy I was treating. The cashier looked at him, then gave me sort of a worried look. I didn't know why he gave me such a look at the time, but I think I figured it out later.

I'm sure it was right of me to buy the fellow some food, but it may have been wrong to have made it an all-you-can-eat affair. You see, he was still eating when we left. Although that may not have been a contributing factor, when I drove by the same restaurant just a few days later, there was a sign that read: *Closed. Out of Business.*

55

Ha-Ha

SAMMY

*V*icki and I were watching a movie last night about a tour guide in Greece. In one scene, the guide was commenting about the kind of folks that often make up a tour.

She noted that Canadians were usually nice while Americans were demanding. She said there would always be a happily married couple as well as some just divorced folks, etc. She then pointed at a man and said, "And there is always one of those guys. The man who thinks he is so funny and drives everyone crazy."

When Vicki heard that, she almost split her sides laughing. And I knew why. That guy is me.

Now let me say, if it is just you and me, I can be pretty serious. I'll actually carry on a fairly intelligent conversation. But add one more person to the mix, and I suddenly become *on*. So I don't show my serious side very often. This was proven at a luncheon my wife attended when someone said, "You know, Vicki's husband is really a pretty smart guy."

To which a lady who knew me asked incredulously, "He is?"

I don't know why I'm the way I am. I know sometimes/most of the time/all of the time, I go overboard. I really don't mean to, but I just see things differently than most folks. I talk and words just start coming out I hadn't even thought about. Some think what I say is funny. Some roll their eyes and let out audible sighs. But, hey, I amuse a few of them. That is enough to keep me going.

I guess I may have developed a sense of humor as a defense mechanism. I didn't have much self-confidence as a youngster. But I learned early-on that if you could make people laugh, they would accept you.

When I was in high school, even the girls seemed to like it as I told my jokes and treated them to my brand of hilarity. They were laughing, but it wasn't all that funny as they giggled their way off with some other guy.

It's not that some folks haven't been good about pointing out my need to pull back a little on the witticisms, or at least pick my spots to use them.

For example, a few years back when I used to make the announcements at church, I would always add a little humor (I thought) and the congregation seemed to enjoy it.

But the preacher? Not so much. He told me that during the announcements, I needed to dispense with the humor. It was disruptive.

As I listened to him, I could almost hear Miss Mildred, my high school English teacher, saying, "Sammy, why don't you use your humor in a creative way such as writing instead of being so disruptive in class?"

That was a hundred years ago. Looks like I would learn.

Another time as we were visiting with friends, my wits were on fire. I was reeling off the quips left and right. As the night wore on, the female friend told Vicki, "I don't know how you live with him. He would drive me crazy."

I'm sorry, Vicki. Is that what happened to you?

I know I get on folk's nerves. I really don't mean to, but I know I do. Sometimes, a person doesn't want a comedy routine. They just want a straight answer to their question or no comment on something they have said. I've told Vicki that I don't want to be one of those guys where people scatter like a covey of quail when he starts walking toward them.

She soothes me by telling me people, especially younger folks, just don't get my humor, anymore. That she is the only one who really understands me—and it's getting harder for her.

So I'm going to try. No promises, but I'm going to try to be a little quieter, maybe a little easier to be around. I want to still have fun and have a good laugh or two, but not at the expense of driving people crazy. And when I need to be motivated to keep trying, I'll just remember the check-out girl at the supermarket.

I was teasing Vicki about something and noticed the girl giving me a disapproving look as she scanned our groceries.

"Look, Vicki," I said, referring to the girl, "she isn't laughing."

"That," the girl replied, "is because you *ain't* funny."

56

Laughing Out Loud

VICKI

I have a bone to pick with Sammy Griffis, the author of the last chapter, titled *Ha-Ha*. I take great umbrage when someone says things like that about my husband, even if that person happens *to be* my husband.

You see, I love his humor. That is what sets him apart from any other person I have ever met. And just to remind him, he didn't watch *this* girl walking off with some other guy. I walked off with *him*. It wasn't exactly love at first sight, so I had to walk by him again. And I have to admit, it was one of the greatest decisions of my life.

Funny, he said no one thought he was funny. My family thinks he is hysterical. You see, every year our family sends out a question-naire to answer for our family reunion booklet. His answers keep everyone giggling.

Question: "What book are you currently reading?"
Sammy: *How to Avoid Panic Attacks Even When She Has the Remote Control.*

(Of course there is no book by that name, but hey, maybe he should write one.)

Question: "What is your favorite TV show?"

Sammy: *Dog Eat Dog* on the Game Show Network. I like it because of the physical and mental challenges of the show. It has absolutely nothing to do with the host of the show being the hottest female (her age, of course) on the face of the earth.

Question: When you need to lose a few pounds, what is the best way for you to do it?

Sammy: Lie.

Question: What do you do when you're embarrassed? Laugh? Cry? Blush? Etc?

Sammy: I Usually Etc.

Question: What is one thing you have done in the last year that you are especially pleased about?

Sammy: Remained alive.

Question: What is your favorite place to read and why?

Sammy: Bathroom. I enjoy multi-tasking.

Question: What is your favorite Walt Disney movie, and why do you like it?

Sammy: *Old Yeller*. I don't know, I guess I am just a sucker for romantic movies.

And our friends think he is funny. When he recently described a vacation during conversations back and forth on the alumni site, one of his fans on the site wrote that he should have been a stand-up comedian. Sammy's version of a great vacation which elicited that observation is as follows:

Vicki and I went all the way to Sherman (thirty-five miles from home. Can you believe it?) We visited Ross, Target, and a bookstore.

Later as we continued on our trip, we dined at the upscale restaurant, Cheddars. (Hey, we were on vacation and I spare no expense to show my Little Vicki a good time.)

Too soon it was time for the journey back home, so I kicked the tires, checked the oil, plugged in the GPS and began the long trip back to Celeste.

The excitement didn't stop when we left Sherman, however. I had one more surprise for Little Vicki. Imagine, if you can, the joy she felt when I (on a spontaneous impulse) whipped into the Sonic right outside Bells and let her order a chicken strip Kid's Meal. The toy that came with the meal will be a memento of our trip she will cherish forever.

We finally arrived home tired, but very satisfied with our exotic vacation. Sherman is on the outer edge of my comfort zone, but I am glad I threw caution to the wind to experience this awesome adventure. I only hope I haven't set the bar too high for all the other husbands out there. Please don't compare them to me. I am one in a million.

Now, Mr. Sammy Griffis, that is funny, I don't care who you are!

57

Night Owls And Early Birds

SAMMY

They say opposites attract. I say they are right. Although Vicki and I share a lot of the same interests and thoughts, we are definitely as different as night and day in several ways.

Take traveling for instance. We don't think exactly alike on that subject. At my age, when someone says, "Go," I immediately head for the bathroom—Vicki heads for the car. She doesn't care where we are going. She just wants to go.

I can't imagine ever doing this—but let's say, I asked Vicki if she wanted to take an auto trip to New York City with her doing the driving. She would immediately jump up, pack about twelve suitcases and be under the steering wheel in two minutes, ready to go. We would get to about the end of the driveway when she would turn to me and ask, "Now, which way is New York?"

I'm a little different. I would change the oil, check the tires, belts and every other thing I could think of on the vehicle. When I finished all that, I would spend time figuring out which route would be the best, how long it would take, etc. Then I would pack my gym bag, cram it in between the suitcases and begin the trip. Oh, yeah, I would also consider everything that could possibly go wrong. Vicki loves me for that. She says she never has to worry. I do enough for both of us.

Vicki is much more outgoing than I. I have to know someone for a while before I warm up to them, but she never meets a stranger. She can walk into a room full of people she has never met, and in five minutes, it's as if they were all lifelong friends. She's also a hugger. Hasn't seen you in a while? Hug. Having problems? Hug. Accomplish something? Hug. Need to leave the room to use the bathroom? Hug.

I used to caution her about hugging everyone. I told her it might make some folks uncomfortable. I changed my mind, though, when the wife of an elderly client stopped by our business one day.

She came in to tell Vicki she was bringing her husband home from the hospital. But before going on home, he wanted to stop by our office. "He's out in the car and wants to see you," she told Vicki. This was not unusual, as Vicki often went out to customer's cars to get their payments, changes, or just to say, "Hi."

Well, this day, Vicki went out to the car and asked the gentleman what she could do for him. He told her, "Vicki, I'm not doing too well, and I just needed one of your hugs."

She gave him a big hug, and just for good measure, gave his wife one, too.

One commonality Vicki and I do share is shopping. However, our modus operandi differs somewhat. I look around a while, make a few selections and am good to go. Not her. She feels a need to pick up and examine almost every item in the store. Finally, after an excruciatingly long passage of time and a cart full of merchandise, I'll think she is headed toward the front to check out. But no-o-o.

She points to the clothes in the cart and indicates she is going to try on all of them.

"All of them—as in every one of them?" I ask. She nods in the affirmative. My heart sinks and my blood pressure rises as I realize it will be another long delay before we leave the store. *Why?* I ask myself. *Why do I even come along? I know this is going to happen every time.*

I guess the answer is I enjoy being with her. Yeah, it's true I like listening to music while she prefers talk radio. She's a night owl. I'm an early bird. She has an insatiable curiosity which makes reading and the internet almost addictive to her. Me? I don't need all that. I'm blessed to already know just about everything there is to know.

Still, despite our differences, there is no one I would rather be with. We pretty much have given up trying to mold each other into what we think the other one should be. I am who I am, and she is who she is. I'm pretty sure this late in the game, that's the way it's going to stay.

But since I'm on the subject, "Vicki, it probably wouldn't hurt if you. . .nah, don't go changing for me. I love you just the way you are."

Part Six

. . . . And A Side Of Snickers!

Genesis 21:6
God has made laughter for me; everyone
who hears will laugh with me.

58

Happy, Happy, Happys

VICKI

Take a moment and share a few laughs from Sammy and me. . .and ones my witty family and friends have said or laughed about. . .and a few posts that I wish I knew who the author was because you kept us laughing at things we wish we had thought up.

1. I just got called a pretty young lady from a 95-year-old man. Guess who just brought sexy back?

2. Well, maybe I brought sexy backwards.

3. According to customer service, I can't bring sexy back—without the receipt—apparently.

4. I do try to keep in shape. Why, I just did a bunch of crunches and curls. They were Nestlé Crunches and cheese curls; but still, I'm exhausted.

5. My fitness goal is to weigh what I told the DMV I weigh.

6. It started this morning with my daily mantra: I will not eat a donut. . .I will not eat a donut. . .I will not eat. . .I will not eat a third donut. . .I will not eat a third donut.

7. My New Year's resolution was to lose thirty pounds by the end of the year. I only have forty more to go.

8. I just got finished doing five sets of diddly squats.

9. I do all my own stunts, but rarely intentionally.

10. My doctor told me that jogging would add ten years to my life. She's right! I feel ten years older already!

11. Oh, well, I never thought I'd be the type of person who would get up early in the morning to exercise—I was right.

12. Guys, complaining about your wife's talking will result in having to sit through her talk about the time you complained about her talking.

13. Apparently walking up behind a guy in the produce aisle with celery in my hand and saying, "I'm stalking you," was way funnier in my head.

14. My daughter told me my grandkids are becoming obsessed with computer games, and that while they are at my house, I need to work with them on it. I'm like, "I do—I'm player #2."

15. Me this a.m.: Go out for breakfast?
    Him: Sure!

Me: Ok, let me shower first. Showers, dresses, changes clothes, dresses, puts on makeup. . . .
Him: Where should we go for lunch?

16. Him: My wife complains that I never open the car door for her, but when I do she's all, "Stop it, you're driving too fast! We're on a bridge!"

17. Watching Hoarders makes me look around my house and say, "Hey! At least all of my cats are alive."

18. I hear about all those wives who can do everything, and I think—hey, I should have them do some stuff for me!

19. I tried killing a spider with hairspray. He's still alive, but his hair looks amazing!

20. We will never forget the Ice Storm of 2014. Sammy has it so cold in here I think I am going to have to salt the hallway.

21. Could be worse. In 1967, it was ten degrees, and I was walking to school in the ice and snow. . .uphill, both ways!

22. During these cold spells, there are many different ways one can save energy—I normally use the recliner.

23. You aren't considered elderly until you've been caught rinsing off a paper plate.

24. If you're wondering about my cooking skills, I've been asked to bring only paper towels to my grandson's graduation party.

25. You guys know I'm not one to brag, but my cooking is to die from.

26. Guys, you let women in the military, but say you don't know if they can fight on the front lines. All the general has to do is walk over to the women and say, "You see the enemy over there? They say you look fat in those uniforms." Mission accomplished!

27. Guys, when she stops crying and gets really quiet, keep your guard up. You're experiencing what scientists refer to as "The eye of the storm."

28. Guys, if your wife asks you, "What would you do without me?"
"Live happily ever after," is not the correct answer.

29. I'm gonna say skydiving is probably not for me since I just screamed when the toilet seat shifted.

30. Look, little Missy, before you debate with me, just remember I have been around the block a few times—I forgot where I lived—but hey—just saying!

31. Listen, I'm a girly girl. So please don't ask me what a transmission is—because I don't know anything about sports.

32. I've often wondered what an atheist would do if stuck behind a car that wasn't moving at a green light, and had a bumper sticker on it that read, "Honk if you love Jesus."

33. The difference in our grandmother's kitchen and our kitchens:

Our grandmothers put their pies on the windowsill to cool. We put our pies on the windowsill to thaw.

34. I don't mind going to work. It's that eight-hour wait to go home that bugs me. I don't work on days that end with Y.

35. Seriously, one day I am going to retire and live off my savings. What I am going to do the second day I have no idea!

36. Speaking of savings, my bank lets me send a text message, and it'll text back with my balance. It's a cool feature, but I didn't think the LOL was necessary.

37. My bucket list:

    2 drumsticks
    4 wings
    1 corn on the cob
    1 biscuit
    1 fried pie

    Extra crispy

38. Am I the only one who watches their garage door close completely just in case a murderer rolls under there at the last minute?

39. I think they should offer free bungee jumps for Congress, no strings attached.

40. I've never been skydiving, but I have zoomed in on Google Earth really, really fast.

41. I just bought another 8-pack of toilet paper. Well, that's another $10 down the toilet.

42. A friend in Sunday School: Sammy, what are you doing after church?

    Sammy: I am doing what the little voices inside Vicki's head tell me to do.

43. Everyone else can have runny noses, their eyes shut, or food in their teeth; but if I look skinny, it is a great group photo.

44. Most awkward moment—when I was checking in the window of the car parked beside me to see if my lipstick was smeared and realized there was someone inside.

45. I went to the store this morning and asked for $5 worth of gas. The clerk burped and handed me a receipt.

46. Dear Lord, please forgive me for the words I said in hunger.

47. Every guy thinks a girl's perfect dream is to meet the perfect guy. Psh! Every girl's dream is to eat whatever she wants and not get fat.

48. I like to eat healthy, but we all know what happened that time Eve ate fruit. Best not to risk it.

49. You can tell a lot from a woman's hands. If they are around your neck, you have probably ticked her off.

50. Marriage—betting someone half your stuff that they will love you forever.

51. Whatever you do, always give 100%—unless you are donating blood.

52. *The Wizard of Oz* is the ultimate chick-flick—two women trying to kill each other over shoes!

53. Winked at someone today and got handed a bottle of Visine. So you could say I know a thing or two about flirting.

54. I got gas yesterday for $1.79—gotta love pinto beans.

55. Husband says if a man says he'll fix it, he will. There is no need to remind him every 6 months about it.

56. It is important to have a twinkle in your wrinkles.

57. Life is short—smile while you still have teeth.

58. Yesterday I fell down a 14-step ladder—lucky I was on the second step.

59. There is no excuse for laziness. But if you find one, let me know!

60. Me: Honey, you are really cute without your glasses.
    Him: Honey, you are really cute without my glasses.

61. All I ask is that if I am murdered, you make my chalk outline four sizes smaller.

62. We are so broke this New Year's Eve, we are gonna party like it's $19.99.

63. Menopause, this is the hottest I have been in years!

64. Do you brush your teeth without making a mess like in the commercial—because I usually look like I have minty fresh rabies.

65. Right now I'm having amnesia and déjà vu at the same time— I think I have forgotten this before.

66. I am going to work out to Wii Fit in the a.m. Not bragging— I just want you to know where to send the ambulance.

67. I saw an atheist friend of mine at TGIF. . .did he or didn't he?

68. I scream. . .you scream. . .we all scream. Those Mexican restaurant restroom gender signs were unclear.

69. Removing makeup—or as I like to say, "Resetting face to factory settings."

70. Ladies, the best way to get your husbands to do something is to suggest they are too old to do it. You're welcome!

71. Never go to a combination dentist/proctologist—but if you do, get the dental work first.

72. I just caught Sammy smiling in his sleep. He is going to pay for that later.

73. I might wake up early and go running, or I might win the lottery. The odds are about the same.

74. If it doesn't make you afraid to go to the bathroom the next day—it's not really hot sauce.

75. Is your GPS supposed to sigh before it says, "Recalculating?"

76. Someone asked me if I had lived in Celeste all my life. I said, "Not yet!"

77. This guy at the gym just did three sets of selfies.

78. I don't like to brag, but I am *Wheel of Fortune* smart.

79. Just realized I am still on my starter marriage.

80. It is that time of year again to reflect and remember why I love my tax deductions. . .kids. . .I meant kids!

81. I was always afraid I would wind up in the gutter. I just didn't know everyone would keep on bowling.

82. Even if I am mad at Sammy, I should be mature enough not to flush the toilet on purpose while he's in the shower. . .but it turns out I am not.

83. As soon as the doctor made me put on one of those little gowns, I knew the end was in sight.

84. Some kids stay out of trouble because they know better. My kids stay out of trouble because they know me.

85. My brain has too many tabs open.

86. When I die, I am leaving my body to science fiction.

87. When I was young, and it got cold, the three of us kids slept in one bed. When it got colder, Mama threw on another sister.

88. When I was little, we had a sand box. It was a quicksand box. I was an only child. . .eventually.

89. I've never been locked up—but I did get stuck in a pair of skinny jeans at Old Navy once.

90. Landlords who don't allow dogs, but do allow children, don't know very much about children.

91. Sammy in Sunday School: I don't know what is wrong with me today.
    Me: Oh, Oh—Pick me, Pick me—I know!

92. My heart says, "Eat those donuts," but my jeans say, "For the love of God, Woman, eat some salad!"

93. Ladies, when your husband is talking to a pretty girl, let him—just to see how many minutes he can hold his stomach in.

94. I have to be funny because being hot is no longer an option.

95. Sammy: Vicki, I notice you aren't yourself today—I really like it.

96. You never know what you have—until you clean your room.

97. Sammy: Vicki, please try to act normal today.
    Me: You are going to have to be more specific.

98. Sammy says he wants to bring me back to reality—like I have been there before.

99. Sammy says I can suffer in silence louder than anyone he knows!

100. Sammy: Your honor, I would like to plead insanity.
     Judge: On what grounds?
     Sammy: I am married to Vicki.
     Judge: I will allow it.